Battleships of the U.S. Navy in World War II

Battleships of the U.S. Navy in World War II

with 115 detailed drawings by
Siegfried Beyer and 148 photographs

Stefan Terzibaschitsch

translated and adapted by
Heinz O. Vetters and Richard Cox

BONANZA BOOKS • NEW YORK

©*J.F. LEHMANNS VERLAG, MUNICH 1977*

Library of Congress Cataloging in Publication Data

Terzibaschitsch, Stefan.
    Battleships of the U. S. Navy in World War II.

    Translation of Die Schlachtschiffe der US-Navy im 2.
Weltkrieg.
      Bibliography: p.
      Includes index.
      1. Battleships. 2. United States. Navy. 3. World
War, 1939-1945—Naval operations, American. I. Title.
V767.T4613   940.54'59'73   77-11163
ISBN 0-517-23451-3

This edition is published by Bonanza Books
a division of Crown Publishers, Inc.
by arrangement with Thornton Cox Publishers

Table of Contents

Acknowledgments

The author wishes to express his thanks to Mr. Volker Schwartz of J. F. Lehmanns, Publishers, and Mr. Heinz O. Vetters for their help in creating this edition and to Mr. Siegfried Breyer for the use of his drawings. He also owes thanks to Professor Dr. Jurgen Rohwer for permission to work in the archives of his library in Stuttgart. Finally for help with the all important photographic documentation his thanks are due to:

The office of Naval Information, Department of the Navy, Washington, D.C.
The United States Naval Institute, Annapolis, Md.
Messrs. G. Albrecht, A. Barilli, W. H. Davis, A. Fraccaroli, W. Globke, N. Polmar, and Fr. Villi.

Stefan Terzibaschitsch
Leonberg
Summer 1977

Introduction

The Organisation of the U.S. Battleship Fleet.

During World War II U.S. battleships were organised in *Battleship Divisions* (BATDIV) with three to four ships in each Division. In the framework of pre-war strategic planning the BATDIV was a tactical unit, as were units of other types of warships. It was composed of ships of one class or—in the case of classes containing only two ships, like the *Nevada*, *Pennsylvania* and *Tennessee* classes—of similar ones. Besides tactical considerations there were many other reasons for selecting similar ships to form a unit: logistics, administration, training, speeds and ranges of action.

During the pre-war years the composition of the BATDIVs changed little. The newcomers *Washington* and *North Carolina* did not join the Fleet until 1941. In the years before the war there were four active BATDIVs (two *Pennsylvania* class plus *Nevada*; two *Tennessee* class plus *Oklahoma*; three *New Mexico* class; and three *Colorado*). Additionally there was a training unit incorporating the older battleships.

The outbreak of war changed much within this organisation. The attack on Pearl Harbor brought the total loss of two battleships and disabled others, and a new tactical concept reduced the pre-war BATDIV, with its permanently attached ships, to more or less an administrative unit. Instead the Task Group (TG) became the characteristic operational wartime unit. Normally having a Rear Admiral as Task Group Commander, the TG had a variable composition depending on its operational tasks. It might for example include transports or minesweepers. Within a TG there could be not only warships detached from their units, but complete divisions or squadrons of certain types of ships. In the later war years the Task Groups were divided into Task Units of differing composition.

The Task Group was a unit within the Task Force (TF), normally commanded by a Vice Admiral. A Task Force consisted of two or more Task Groups, while the ships of the Task Forces within a given operational area were designated a Fleet and commanded by an Admiral.

Pennant (hull) Numbers and Nomenclature

Every vessel of the U.S. Navy is given a number prior to construction (hull number), this being a distinctive serial number, prefaced by initials denoting the category to which she belongs. With the completion of the ship this number becomes the pennant number. Before the war this distinctive number was carried by destroyers and smaller vessels only, painted on both sides of the bow. With the outbreak of war, the large-sized numbers were replaced by smaller ones in order to make the identity of the ship less recognizable, but it is known that even the small-sized numbers were visible by enemy submarines under favourable conditions. During the war all battleships and cruisers also had their respective numbers painted on both sides of the bow and in some cases on both sides of the fantail too. Sometime after the war this system was replaced by standardized large-sized white numbers with black outlines on both sides of the bow, occasionally repeated in a smaller size on both sides of the fantail.

With one exception all the battleships of the U.S. Navy were named after Federal States. During the fifty years and more of the battleship era every federal state's name was carried by at least one battle-ship, whether built or only planned. Records show that names of some states were used twice (e.g. *South Dakota*, *Washington*) or even three times (e.g. *Iowa*) in the long list of U.S. battleships. An exception to this rule of nomenclature was made with the planned battlecruisers of 1916/20, called after historic battles or other evocative names. These were later used for aircraft carriers (*Lexington, Saratoga, Ranger*).

This tradition has not been lost. By the mid-1970s there were only four battleships of the *Iowa* class left in the reserve fleet, but the practice of naming after Federal States has been carried on with the heavy nuclear-powered frigates (DLGN), in fact the size of cruisers. The first was the type ship DLGN 36 *California* followed by *South Carolina* (DLGN 37), *Virginia* (DLGN 38), *Texas* (DLGN 39), *Arkansas* (DLGN 40) and *Mississippi* (DLGN 41)—all previously famous battleship names. The two predecessors within this category of nuclear-powered frigates (DLGN 25) *Bainbridge* and (DLGN 35) *Truxtun* and all other conventional-powered frigates DLG and DL were named after famous naval officers. On July 1, 1975 all DLG and DLGN ships were reclassified as cruisers and given the initials CG and CGN respectively. Within the category of cruisers were also the

original "old" cruisers named after large cities (four of these were still in active service at the time of writing).

Lost and Damaged Battleships

Of the eight battleships at Pearl Harbor on December 7, 1941, two—*Arizona* and *Oklahoma*—were sunk, and the other six suffered medium to heavy damage. *Oklahoma* was righted and re-floated in 1943 but found not worth rebuilding. *Arizona* and *Oklahoma* were the only total war losses among U.S. battleships; the war losses of the other sea powers (Germany, Japan, Soviet Union, Great Britain, France, Italy) were much higher.

Some U.S. battleships were badly damaged in the war, but with their sturdy construction and the later strengthening of hulls and superstructures they were able to withstand the punishment without becoming

Names of U.S. Battleships

PN	Name		PN of former ships		PN	Name			
	Texas	BB 35 b.	CGN 39		BB 26	South Carolina	—	CGN 37	
	Maine	BB 10 b.	BB 69 canc		BB 27	Michigan	—	SSBN 727	
BB 1	Indiana	BB 50 pl.	BB 58 b.		BB 28	Delaware	—	—	
BB 2	Massachusetts	BB 54 pl.	BB 59 b.		BB 29	North Dakota	—	—	
BB 3	Oregon	—	—		BB 30	Florida	—	—	BM 9
BB 4	Iowa	BB 53 pl.	BB 61 b.		BB 31	Utah	—	—	
BB 5	Kearsarge	—	CV 33		BB 32	Wyoming	—	—	BM 10
BB 6	Kentucky	—	BB 66 canc		BB 33	Arkansas	—	CGN 41	BM 7
BB 7	Illinois	—	BB 65 canc		BB 34	New York	—	—	CA 2
BB 8	Alabama	—	BB 60 b.		BB 36	Nevada	—	—	BM 8
BB 9	Wisconsin	—	BB 64 b.		BB 37	Oklahoma	—	—	
BB 11	Missouri	—	BB 63 b.		BB 38	Pennsylvania	—	—	CA 4
BB 12	Ohio	—	BB 68 canc SSBN 726 b.		BB 39	Arizona	—	—	
					BB 40	New Mexico	—	—	
BB 13	Virginia	—	CGN 38		BB 43	Tennessee	—	—	CA 10
BB 14	Nebraska	—	—		BB 44	California	—	CGN 36	CA 6
BB 15	Georgia	—	—		BB 45	Colorado	—	—	CA 7
BB 16	New Jersey	—	BB 62 b.		BB 46	Maryland	—	—	CA 8
BB 17	Rhode Island	—	—		BB 47	Washington	n.compl.	BB 56 b.	
BB 18	Connecticut	—	—		BB 48	West Virginia	—	—	CA 5
BB 19	Louisiana	—	BB 71 canc		BB 49	South Dakota	pl.	BB 57 b.	CA 9
BB 20	Vermont	—	—		BB 51	Montana	pl.	BB 67 canc.	CA 13
BB 21	Kansas	—	—		BB 52	North Carolina	pl.	BB 55 b.	CA 12
BB 22	Minnesota	—	—						
BB 23	Mississippi	BB 41 b.	CGN 40						
BB 24	Idaho	BB 42 b.	—						
BB 25	New Hampshire	—	BB 70 canc						

48 Federal States (except Kearsarge)

abbreviations:
b.	*— built*
pl.	*— planned*
canc.	*— cancelled*
n. compl.	*— not completed*

total losses. In 1946 the old battleships *Arkansas, New York, Nevada* and *Pennsylvania* were used in the target fleet for the nuclear tests off Bikini, and destroyed.

The Ships' Aircraft

The advantages of aerial scouting were clearly realized by all navies during and after World War I. By the end of the 1920's U.S. battleships and cruisers were equipped with one or two catapults and were equipped with three to four light seaplanes for aerial reconnaissance. Up to the cessation of war in 1945 the following aircraft were in use on U.S. ships:

Vought "Corsair"	03U	introduced 1927
Keystone	OL9	introduced 1930
Curtiss "Seagull"	SOC	introduced 1934
Vought "Kingfisher"	OS2U-1	introduced 1941
Curtiss "Seagull"	SO-3C	introduced 1942
Curtiss "Seahawk"	SC-1	introduced 1944

The introduction of long range radar and the increasing practice of giving task forces and task groups aircraft carriers made the carriage of seaplanes on board battleships and cruisers less and less necessary. The reconnaissance potential of carrier-borne aircraft was far greater and they suffered none of the operational limitations of the seaplanes, which had to land on the sea close to a battleship and be hoisted aboard by crane. Furthermore the handling gear, stowage space and highly inflammable aviation fuel required by the seaplanes were always a handicap in fighting ships designed to carry guns. When World War II ended the seaplanes with their catapults and handling equipment were finally removed from all battleships and cruisers. The space thus released was used for the newly introduced helicopters, or in some ships for the stowage of boats.

Ships' Colour Schemes

With some exceptions battleships in pre-war years were painted in two basic colours: haze gray or pale gray for all vertical surfaces, including the tops of gun turrets, and dark blue (deck blue) for all horizontal surfaces, excepting wooden decks, which were varnished. This paint scheme was returned to after the war. During the war battleships were sometimes painted in camouflage like other ships. Depending on the ship's silhouette, and the way it was desired to disguise this, various standardised schemes called 'measures' were applied.

The primary tasks of ship-borne planes included reconnaissance; air observation and control of gun fire; search for, and rescue of, aircraft crews downed over the sea; liaison, courier, and messenger missions. The seaplanes were launched from catapults. On their return from missions they had to be picked up and hoisted aboard without interfering too much with the ship's fighting capability. The standard equipment of major ships included three or four such seaplanes. The photograph shows an OS2U (Kingfisher) seaplane positioned on the catapult aboard the memorial ship BB 60 *Alabama*.   Photo USS *Alabama* Battleship Commission

Measure 2: "graded system" with hull in ocean gray, vertical surfaces of the superstructure in haze gray, top of director tower in pale gray, deck blue for all decks and horizontal surfaces.

Measure 12: hull and superstructure in an ocean gray base coat with irregular splashes of navy blue.

Measure 21: "navy blue system", all vertical surfaces in navy blue and all decks in deck blue.

Measure 22: "graded system", hull in navy blue from waterline to the lowest point of sheer, hull above this level and superstructure in haze gray, decks in deck blue.

Measure 32: "medium pattern system", dazzle-painted in pale gray, haze gray and navy blue to a pattern, and deck blue applied on all decks and horizontal surfaces.

Measure 13: Normal peacetime system in haze gray.

There are some indications that ships with wooden decks received a deck-blue coat for their decks during the war. All paints used were matte to avoid reflecting light.

Radar Antennas

Many years before the U.S.A. entered the war some ships of the U.S. Navy were already equipped with radar. It is not within the scope of this book to deal with all the technical and operational details of all the different radar systems. The following information is limited to antennas with their designations:

XAF A large-sized rectangular antenna, first installed in BB *New York* in 1938 and later removed.

CXZ An antenna similar to XAF, installed in BB *Texas* in 1938 and later removed.

CX-AM Installed in 1940/41 in some of the older battleships and later removed.

SC A rectangular antenna with a greater width.

SRa A small-sized longish antenna shaped as an inverted V, installed in older battleships; some arrangements with two antennas were known.

SG A small-sized navigational and surface search antenna of no significance in ships' recognition, therefore only occasionally mentioned.

SK A large rectangular aircraft interception antenna, known in two different patterns—with and without headpiece. By the end of the war it had been partly replaced by SK-2 antennas.

SC-2 A small-sized rectangular elongated antenna with headpiece, mainly used on carriers, destroyers and escorts, rarely in battleships and cruisers.

SK-2 A large round parabolic antenna with wide open-work metal grating, which had replaced SK in most battleships, cruisers and aircraft carriers by the end of the war.

SP A smaller-sized round parabolic antenna with closer grating, introduced in the last part of the war as a secondary antenna system, always carried in an aft position.

SG-6 One of the first post-war antennas, installed in limited numbers only and soon replaced by the newly introduced SPS-6.

SPS-6 One of the first larger air-search antennas of the SPS- series. Introduced in post-war years and installed in numerous ships including some of other navies, where it is still in use. Ships of the *Iowa* class were the only battleships equipped with the SPS-6.

SPS-8A　The "highfinder" surveillance radar system, installed in ships of the *Iowa* class around 1950, replacing the SP; a somewhat older but similar version was fitted in AG 128 *Mississippi* in 1949, as well as in some aircraft carriers.

The short descriptions of each ship later in this book refer to the above radar antennas as important ship recognition indicators.

Torpedo armament

All the older battleships, including the ships of the *Colorado* class, were originally equipped with two to four underwater torpedo tubes of 21 in. (53.5 cm) caliber. However, these tubes were removed during refit periods up to about 1935. Ships of the *North Carolina* and following classes never had torpedo tubes.

Guns

The following table shows all the guns mounted in the completed battleships which are described in this book. In the early fifties it was planned to replace all 40 mm A.A. guns with a new model 3.5 in (7.6 cm) 450 D.P. gun in twin-mountings, but this was never done. The many 20 mm A.A. guns in service were reduced in numbers after the war and were finally removed when the Korean war ended. A number of 28 mm L/75 A.A. guns, installed on some ships before the war, proved to be ineffective and were quickly replaced by 40 mm L/60 Bofors guns. The 28 mm's are therefore not mentioned in the following table.

Technical data.

All the important data on ships covered by this book is summed up in tables. A predominant part of the figures listed are taken out of the book

Guns installed on U.S. battleships

Caliber cm.	inch	Barrel length in calibers	designation	year of construction	range at maximum elevation (km)/°	Rate of fire rounds/min.	weight of turret ts	Used in
		Heavy guns						
40,6	16	L/45	Mark 15	1910	31,0/30°	1,5	1.245	Colorado Class; in addition: Mark 5 and Mark 8 turrets
40,6	16	L/45	Mark 6	1936	37,1/45°	2	1.437	North Carolina, South Dakota class
40,6	16	L/50	Mark 7	1936	38,7/45°	2	1.708	Iowa class
35,6	14	L/45	Mark 2	1911	30,0/30°	1,5	864*	*Twin-turret New York, Oklahoma and Pennsylvania class
35,6	14	L/50	Mark 4	1915	32,5/30°	1,5	1.127	New Mexico and Tennessee class
30,5	12	L/50	Mark 7	1910	21,5/15°		607	Wyoming Class
		Medium guns						
12,7	5	L/51	Mark 15	1907	17,2/45°	7	in casemates	Wyoming through Maryland class
		A.A. guns						
12,7	5	L/25	Mark 13	1923	13,2/85°	6	open mount	Nevada through Maryland class
12,7	5	L/38	Mark 12	1935	16,1/80°	10	30-twin mount 18-single mount	Arkansas, Nevada, Pennsylvania, West Virginia, Tennessee class
7,6	3	L/50	Mark 10	1917	16,3/.	10	open mount	BB 32-48
4,0	1.57	L/60		1942	10.1/85°	150	in quadruple mounts	Used on all ships during WW II
2,0	0.8				5,0/87°	450	single mount	Used on all ships during WW II

"Schlachtschiffe und Schlachtkreuzer 1905–1970" by Siegfried Breyer, while other data derives from U.S. publications.

Plans

All the plans were drawn by S. Breyer on a scale of 1:1250 and were first published in the book "Schlachtschiffe und Schlachtreuzer 1905–1970", published by J. F. Lehmanns Verlag.

Photographs

Most of these are U.S. Navy official photographs. The year they were taken is indicated and photographs from sources other than the U.S. Navy are acknowledged.

One of the first shipboard radar antennas of the U.S. Navy was called XAF. 25 ft wide and 19 ft high, it was installed on the USS *New York* (BB 34) in December 1938 and tested in the course of 1939. The photograph shows this specific antenna carried by a Navy crane ship to the Naval Museum of the Washington Navy Yard.   Photo 8/1964

The U.S. Battleship Fleet at the Outbreak of War with Japan

By December 7, 1941 at the time the Japanese attacked the U.S. Fleet at Pearl Harbor, the European Nations had already been at War for two years. At the outbreak of hostilities in Europe, naval power was still rated in units of battleships available. Six months before the Japanese attacked Pearl Harbor, the fight between the German battleship *Bismarck* and the British *Hood* and *Prince of Wales* ended with the loss of the *Hood*. But the chase by superior British surface forces which ensued with battleships, cruisers and destroyers as well as carrier aircraft, revealed the capabilities of air power in sea warfare. The *Bismarck* was finally sunk with the help of carrierborne aircraft. *Ark Royal's* Swordfish aircraft, considered at the time as being too slow and incapable of playing a decisive role, attacked the *Bismarck* and scored several hits, one of them damaging her propellers and wrecking her steering gear. Thus the most modern and powerful battleship of her time was crippled by torpedoes dropped from aircraft and her fate then sealed by the guns and torpedoes of battleships and cruisers.

The destruction of *Bismarck* marked the last German attempt to use their capital ships without sufficient air cover. At this time it was also recognised that aircraft carriers without accompanying supporting and escorting forces would soon become a target for enemy submarines, and aircraft (note the sinking of the British carriers *Courageous*, *Glorious* and the damage sustained by the *Ark Royal*).

Later events of World War II proved that the policy of maintaining a powerful battleship fleet was justified at this stage, although the future value of aircraft carriers in sea warfare was becoming apparent. The Americans were first confronted with the capability of carrier-based aircraft when the Japanese attacked Pearl Harbor and Japanese dive bombers and torpedo planes swept in to pound the United States Pacific Fleet at anchor in that harbor. Seven battleships were moored in Battleship Row and one was sitting helpless in drydock. Four of them were sunk, the other four damaged. For those not convinced by Pearl Harbor, the Japanese demonstrated the superiority of aircraft three days later, when they attacked and sank the British battleship *Prince of Wales* and the battlecruiser *Repulse* of the British Eastern Fleet, which were operating without fighter cover. The unavoidable lesson of these events

was that the aircraft carrier was a vital component of any force, even though no-one thought the battleship obsolete at that time. But the inclusion of battleships and aircraft carriers in task groups to protect each other was an expensive business. Later, of course, the aircraft carrier appeared as a crucial factor in sea battles, but meanwhile the battleship was still the capital ship to counter the threat of the existing Japanese battleship force or to support amphibious operations with heavy gun fire. Indeed finally, with the installation of numerous antiaircraft guns, battleships became an integral part of carrier groups, providing a badly needed addition to the carriers' own protective antiaircraft fire power. After the war came to an end, the scope for employment of battleships in the future decreased rapidly with the growing introduction of jet aircraft, guided missiles and sophisticated electronics, although the capability of a battleship as a floating gun support battery was clearly demonstrated as late as 1969.

To return to 1941; the Japanese attack on Pearl Harbor was to mark a turning point of U.S. naval building policy. Confused by this spectacular Japanese success, but not demoralized, the Americans made use of their enormous industrial potential and their economic resources. A huge building programme—primarily of aircraft carriers—was implemented by emergency appropriations. Pearl Harbor also hastened the modernization of the U.S. Navy. The damaged battleships entered yards for repairs and modernization, and work on new construction was speeded up. The older battleships left the yards much more powerful than they were prior to being damaged. Thus the attack on Pearl Harbor failed to gain any long term advantages for the Japanese.

The naval building programme rushed in by the Government in 1940 and 1941 for a two-ocean Navy had been sponsored by President F. D. Roosevelt. The objective was a better balance between the U.S. Pacific and Atlantic Fleets and the achievement of a basic defence posture should further developments involve the United States in war. At the time of the Japanese attack on Pearl Harbor, which finally dragged the American nation into the war, the U.S. Pacific and Atlantic Fleets were still far from being balanced, and it was too early for any major units from the new building programme to have joined the

U.S. naval strength. On the eve of the war's outbreak eight of the older battleships—*West Virginia*, *Maryland*, *California*, *Tennessee*, *Pennsylvania*, *Arizona*, *Nevada* and *Oklahoma*—were gathered at Pearl Harbor, with *Colorado* in for a refit at Bremerton; while the Atlantic Fleet mustered eight units with the newcomers *Washington* and *North Carolina*, the *New Mexico*, *Mississippi*, *Idaho*, and the three veterans of World War I—*New York, Texas* and *Arkansas*. The latter, serving as Training Ships, later showed the worth of their fire power in pre-invasion bombardments and as the backbone of valuable convoys. In 1942 *North Carolina* and the three *New Mexico's* left the Atlantic and joined up with the Pacific Fleet. The U.S. battleship fleet entered the war with 17 battleships (against 11 Japanese, including the *Yamato*, placed in commission December 16, 1941). These 17 U.S. battleships could be rated as:

> Two modern to the standards of the end 1930's
> Twelve well armed and protected
> Three obsolete.

The thirteen older battleships had received better protection and more modern A.A. armament during refit and modernization periods in the thirties. But with the outbreak of war it was soon revealed that this A.A. armament did not meet the requirements of modern warfare, and new models of 5 in (12.7 cm) 40 mm and 20 mm guns had to be installed.

Inevitably it is interesting, though academic, to consider the effects of the Washington Treaty on comparative strengths. The twelve units of the *South Dakota I* (battleships) and the *Lexington* (battlecruisers) class plus the BB 47 (*Washington*)—all laid down in 1920/21 and later either scrapped or stopped work on under terms of the Washington Treaty—would have been added to the U.S. Navy's battleship fleet and available in 1941. But equally the Japanese Navy would have been strengthened by the six battleships and eight battlecruisers under construction or planned in 1920/21.

Wartime Documents reveal that the U.S. Navy's strategists had planned to block the enemy's sea lanes and to defend the Central Pacific with strong units of the Pacific Fleet. Meanwhile the Japanese plan for a southward drive to seize the oil supplies of the Dutch East Indies could only be implemented if the U.S. Pacific Fleet was prevented from interfering by a reduction in its superiority. At this time the superiority of naval forces was still reckoned in terms of big ships carrying heavy guns. Therefore the only way the Japanese could hope to eliminate, or at least decimate, this strong U.S. battle fleet was

by a surprise attack: but not an attack by an equally strong battleship force far from its own bases. The weapon chosen was the naval air arm, carried to its take-off position by all the available large fleet carriers and supported by fast battleships, cruisers and destroyers. The risk had to be taken that the force would be detected before its attack could be delivered and some of its carriers lost. But they were not. The strike on Pearl Harbor resulted in the complete immobilization of the U.S. battleship force: it was out of action for many months. Of the eight U.S. battleships bombed and torpedoed six underwent reconstruction and joined the fleet later in the war with more powerful armament, while two damaged beyond repair—*Arizona* and *Oklahoma*—were scrapped.

New battleships under construction or planned had been given a higher priority long before the U.S.A. became involved in the war. So the new *North Carolina* class joined the Fleet in 1941/42. Out of the new building programmes—*South Dakota II*, *Iowa* and *Montana* classes—eight were finally added to the fleet (plus two battlecruisers of the *Alaska* class).

The following table lists all the classes of ships, namely:

Built pre-World War I, during the war, or thereafter, in service at the outbreak of war in 1941.

Planned to be built after World War I.

Built during World War II.

Planned to be built during World War II, but cancelled.

BB	Class	Number of ships planned	commissioned
32-33	Wyoming	2	2
34-35	New York	2	2
36-37	Nevada	2	2
38-39	Pennsylvania	2	2
40-42	New Mexico	3	3
43-44	Tennessee	2	2
45-48	Colorado	4	3
49-54	South Dakota (I)	6	—
CC1-6	Lexington	6	—
55-56	North Carolina	2	2
57-60	South Dakota (II)	4	4
61-66	Iowa	6	4
67-71	Montana	5	—
		46	26

Notes: Of the twenty-six battleships listed, USS *Wyoming* (ex BB 32) was taken out of service in 1932 and was subsequently used as a gunnery training ship (AG 17).

Japanese Battleships 1911-40

The introduction of the British *Dreadnought* battle-ship influenced the ship design of all the major sea-powers prior to World War I. It also launched more than thirty years of competition between the Powers in battleship design, culminating with the ships of the *Bismarck*, *Iowa* and *Yamato* classes. Every attempt by one Power to produce a more powerful class of ship was countered by others trying to surpass it. Interestingly, there was a significant relationship between Japanese and American battleship designs. The following table details this competitive development, showing the number of guns mounted and their calibers.

The *Kongo*, lead ship of the *Kongo* class, built in Great Britain. The photograph shows the *Kongo* after her first reconstruction when her foremast was considerably altered. The unequally high funnels have been given broader edges. The searchlights, later installed upon the platforms abaft the foremost funnel, have not been mounted yet. Note the numerous casemate guns which are—contrary to the American practice—not raised to a more "dry" deck level. Photo August, 1931, Sh. Fukui

Launching dates of U.S. and Japanese battleships

Year	U.S.-Navy date	Name	heavy guns	Japanese Navy date	Name	heavy guns
	launched					
1911	14. 1.	Arkansas	12-12 in.			
	25. 5.	Wyoming	12-12 in.			
1912	18. 5.	Texas	10-14 in.	18. 5.	Kongo	8-14 in.
	30.10.	New York	10-14 in.			
				21.11.	Hiei	8-14 in.
1913				1.12.	Kirishima	8-14 in.
				14.12.	Haruna	8-14 in.
1914	23. 3.	Oklahoma	10-14 in.			
				28. 3.	Fuso	12-14 in.
	11. 7.	Nevada	10-14 in.			
1915	16. 3.	Pennsylvania	12-14 in.			
	19. 6.	Arizona	12-14 in.			
				3.11.	Yamashiro	12-14 in.
1916				12.11.	Ise	12-14 in.
1917				21. 1.	Hyuga	12-14 in.
	25. 1.	Mississippi	12-14 in.			
	23. 4.	New Mexico	12-14 in.			
	30. 6.	Idaho	12-14 in.			
1919	30. 4.	Tennessee	12-14 in.			
				9.11.	Nagato	8-16 in.
	20.11.	California	12-14 in.			
1920	20. 3.	Maryland	8-16 in.			
				31. 5.	Mutsu	8-16 in.
1921	22. 3.	Colorado	8-16 in.			
	19.11.	West Virginia	8-16 in.			
1940	1. 6.	Washington	9-16 in.			
	13. 6.	North Carolina	9-16 in.			
				8. 7.	Yamato	9-18 in.
				1.11.	Musashi	9-18 in.
1941	7. 6.	South Dakota	9-16 in.			
	23. 9.	Massachusetts	9-16 in.			
	21.11.	Indiana	9-16 in.			
1942	16. 2.	Alabama	9-16 in.			
	27. 8.	Iowa	9-16 in.			
	7.12.	New Jersey	9-16 in.			
1943	7.12.	Wisconsin	9-16 in.			
1944	29. 1.	Missouri	9-16 in.			

The *Haruna* on a trial run at 30 knots after her second reconstruction. Her appearance has been completely changed. There are only two funnels left. Her searchlight platforms are placed around the fore funnel. The photograph shows her fully developed "Pagoda" mast and the enlarged aft control tower.   Photo 1933, Sh. Fukui

Between 1911 and 1940 twelve Japanese battleships were launched, comprising one class with four and two classes with two ships each. The following table shows in general the available data relevant to the dates mentioned, but it is not within the scope of this book to note all the alterations in appearance and armament, or the changes in technical features made to Japanese battleships during their service with the fleet. It should be noted that individual ships of single class could differ considerably. Such details are not covered.

The *Fuso* on a trial run after her second reconstruction. She is a highly impressive ship. Her aircraft catapult is placed atop heavy gun turret 3. Note the very high "Pagoda" mast.
Photo 1933, Sh. Fukui

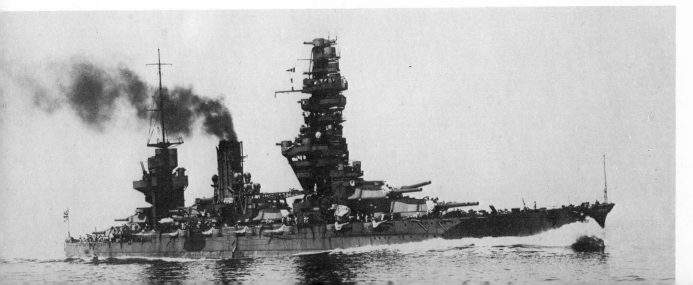

Name	Standard Displacement	Length M.	Beam M.	Draught M.	Engine output/ S.H.P.	Speed Knots
Kongo Class						
Kongo	32.156	219,6	31,0	9,7	136.000	30,5
Hiei ⎫ ca.						
Haruna ⎬ 1937:						
Kirishima ⎭						

All four ships of this class were sunk during World War II: *Kongo* by a submarine in November 1944, *Hiei* by aircraft off Guadalcanal in November 1942, *Haruna* during yard repairs in July 1945, and *Kirishima* by the gunfire of U.S. battleships off Guadalcanal in November 1942.

Name	Standard Displacement	Length M.	Beam M.	Draught M.	Engine output/ S.H.P.	Speed Knots
Fuso Class						
Fuso	34.700	210,0	30,6	9,7	75.000	24,7
Yamashiro						
ca. 1935:						

During the Battle of Leyte in October 1944 *Fuso* and *Yamashiro* were sunk by the gunfire of similarly old U.S. battleships.

Name	Standard Displacement	Length M.	Beam M.	Draught M.	Engine output/ S.H.P.	Speed Knots
Ise Class						
Hyuga	35.800	213,4	31,7	9,2	80.000	25,3
Ise						
ca. 1937:						

Hyuga and *Ise* were destroyed in July 1945 during yard repairs (following damage at the Battle of Leyte) by aircraft from U.S. aircraft carriers.

Name	Standard Displacement	Length M.	Beam M.	Draught M.	Engine output/ S.H.P.	Speed Knots
Nagato Class						
Mutsu	39.130	221,1	34,6	9,5	82.300	25
Nagato						
ca. 1936:						

Mutsu was destroyed by an internal explosion due to an unknown cause in June 1943, *Nagato* survived and was used by the Americans as a nuclear bombing test target ship at Bikini and sunk.

Name	Standard Displacement	Length M.	Beam M.	Draught M.	Engine output/ S.H.P.	Speed Knots
Yamato Class						
Yamato	64.170	256,0	36,9	10,4	150.000	27,0
Musashi						

Both ships were sunk by carrier-borne aircraft: *Musashi* off Leyte in October 1944, *Yamato* off Okinawa in April 1945.

Armament	Armor Thickness in mm horiz.	vert.	Art.	Conning Tower	Complement
8-14 in L/45 14- 6 in L/50 8- 5 in A.A. 20-25 mm A.A. (1940) 3 aircraft	70	76-203	229	152-254	1437
12-14 in L/45 16- 6 in L/50 8- 5 in L/50 16-25 mm A.A. 3 aircraft	32-51	115-305	115-305	135-351	ca.1400
12-14 in L/45 16-5.5 in L/50 8- 5 in A.A. 20-25 mm A.A. 3 aircraft	32-51	76-305	152-305	152-305	1376
8-16 in L/45 18-5.5 in L/50 8- 5 in A.A. 20-25 mm A.A. 3 aircraft	76-178	100-300	356	97-371	1368
9-18 in L/45 12-6.1 in L/55 12- 5 in A.A. 24-25 mm A.A. 4-13 mm A.A. 7 aircraft	30-50	410	250-650	300-500	2500

The *Hyuga* anchored off Kure about one year before Japan entered the war. After several reconstructions there was only one funnel left and a reinforced "Pagoda" mast had been installed. Three airplanes are shown astern.   Photo December 1940, Sh. Fukui

The *Ise* shown after her conversion into a hybrid aircraft carrier. Both her aft turrets were removed and a hangar structure erected instead. The seaplane catapults limited the arcs of fire of her heavy gun turret 4. The medium battery was completely removed. Note the radar antenna atop the range-finder on her fore "Pagoda" mast.   Photo August 1943, Sh. Fukui

Broadside view of the *Mutsu* showing her final appearance after her second reconstruction, when the curving funnel was removed. The photograph shows very clearly her typical casemate gun arrangement.   Photo January 1939, Sh. Fukui

One of the rare complete views of the *Yamato* demonstrating the idiosyncratic design of this ship class. Note the unique shape of her aft hull (bearing the aircraft catapults) the superimposed 6.1 in gun turrets, the heavy 18 in triple-turrets, the inclined funnel, the numerous A.A. gun stations, and the impressive size of the rangefinder on her "Pagoda" mast.

Photo October 1941, Sh. Fukui

Wyoming Class

The launch of the *Dreadnought* in 1906 marked the beginning of a period—the 'Dreadnought era'—of enormous efforts by all the major seapowers to out-flank each other not only in numbers of ships of the line being built but also in ship's design, fire power and armor. Japan, Great Britain, Imperial Germany, France, Italy and Imperial Russia were the competitors. The Americans were not enthusiastic innovators, preferring to adopt progressive features introduced by the other seapowers.

The *Wyoming* class had received as main armament the same 12 in (30.5 cm) caliber guns as its predecessors of the *South Carolina*, *Delaware* and *Florida* classes, although the number of guns was increased by two. While the *South Carolina* class was still equipped with four twin-turrets of this calibre, the *Delaware's* and *Florida's* had five. The addition of a sixth twin-turret in the *Wyoming* class resulted in a weight increase of approximately 4,300 tons and an increase in overall length of 37 ft.

Both *Wyoming* class ships—*Wyoming* and *Arkansas*—were ordered in 1909 and completed in 1912. During 1919 the first series of alterations during a refit took place. Some 5 in guns of the secondary armament mounted in the lower casemates were removed because they had proved inefficient in heavy seas. A variety of pre-war and wartime modifications are shown in the plans and photographs that follow. The main alterations during the 1925/27 refit period were conversion to oil burning, removal of the underwater torpedo tubes, fitting of anti-torpedo bulges, thicker armored decks, and the installation of a catapult on P-turret with handling gear for sea planes. Only *Arkansas* saw active service in World War II. The *Wyoming* had been demilitarised and, after a rebuilding period in 1931, was used as a Gunnery Training Ship (reclassified AG 17).

By the time all the modifications were complete, the full load displacement of *Arkansas* had increased to 31,000 tons, and the ship's appearance changed considerably from her 1919 outline. The former two funnels were trunked into a single upstake, cagemasts replaced by tripods, while the addition of new fire control systems, radar and A.A. guns altered the silhouette of this World War I veteran completely. Other modifications were extensive and could not possibly be listed in detail within the parameter of this book.

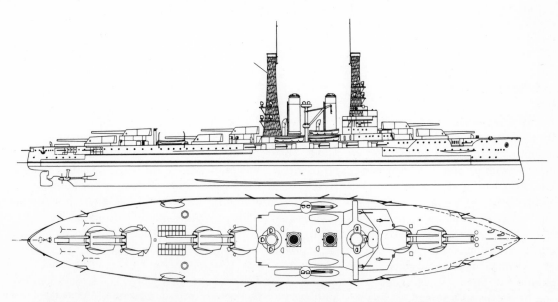

USS *Wyoming* in 1912. There was originally very little space left between her funnels and cage masts. The midship superstructure had not yet been added. In addition to her 5 in L/51 guns in casemate housings she carries other 5 in L/51 guns in open deck mounts and one 5 in L/51 gun in a fantail emplacement.

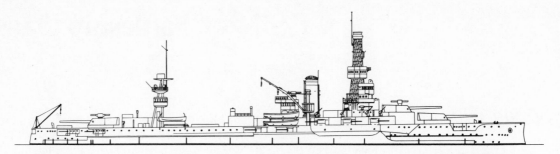

USS *Wyoming* in 1935. The ship was then reclassified AG 17. Note the empty barbettes of her three former heavy gun turrets. The fantail-mounted 5 in gun had been removed. Six of her casemate guns had been mounted one deck higher and A.A. guns added. There was only one single funnel left. Her aft cage mast had been replaced by a tripod mast farther aft.

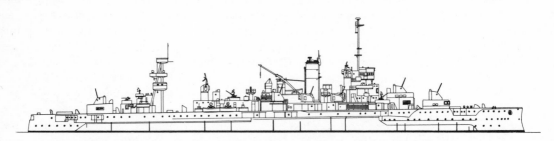

USS *Wyoming* in 1944. The drawing shows her final form after the removal of her fore cage mast. The ship carries 5 in L/51 twin-turrets on old barbettes as well as an open single-mount, two single-turrets and one twin-turret on her starboard side. Mk 37 fire control gear is rigged amidships and on her bridge top. The side armor has been removed.

BB 32 Wyoming (AG 17)

In May 1931 *Wyoming* was "demilitarized", but not totally disarmed. Turrets P, Q, and X of her main armament were removed, and she was re-rated as a "Gunnery Training Ship". During her career in this role she also took part in amphibious exercises. In November 1941 *Wyoming* was again re-rated, this time as an "A.A. Training Ship" and given various models of 5 in guns and guns of smaller calibers, though retaining her main battery of three 12 in gun turrets. All her 5 in casemate guns and the belt armor were removed. The forward cagemast—mounted on top the bridge—was retained. It was not until 1944 that this mast was replaced by a polemast, and the three 12 in gun turrets removed to make space for additional 5 in L/38 guns in twin-mounts. The U.S.

Navy used the designation "twin-mount" for "semi-housed" guns with protective shields, rather than calling them "twin-turrets".

For a long time AG 17 was a trap for anyone preparing ship silhouettes with the aid of only a few available photographs showing the ship's starboard side. The assumption that the port armament was similar to that of the starboard side was not correct. Especially after the modifications at the end of 1941 *Wyoming's* appearance was not symmetrical.

Note: At the same time her classification and number changed to AG 17. The classification initials stand for Miscellaneous Auxiliaries, and most of these AG ships were old ships of the line or ships formerly employed in the fleet train. AG vessels are used for various duties, e.g. for training purposes, as test and as special service ships.

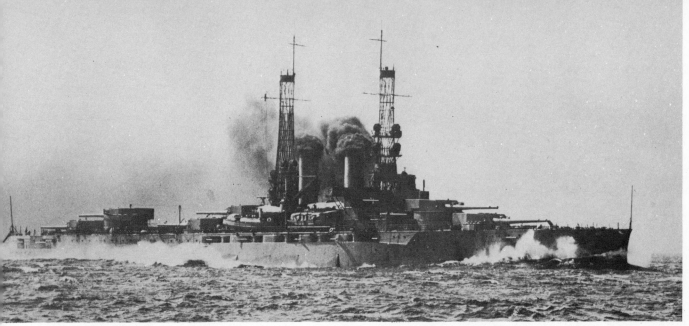

USS *Wyoming* as originally built, during her first years of activation. She still had coal-fired boilers and two funnels. The photograph shows how a choppy sea could impede the operation of her lower casemate guns.

USS *Wyoming* as a Gunnery Training Ship in the 1930's. Rangefinders are mounted on top of her aft gun turret and on the superstructure abaft the funnel. The stern casemate gunport has been plated over. The casemate guns in midships positions have been raised to the upper deck and placed in bays overlapping the ship's sides. The heavy gun turrets in midships position have been removed.

USS *Wyoming* as an A.A. Training Ship. Three of her 12 in gun turrets are still in place. Note the various other guns fitted—5 in guns in twin- and single-enclosed mounts as well as 5 in and 40 mm and 20 mm A.A. guns in open mounts. These are placed asymetrically on the ship's port and starboard sides.   Photo June 1942

USS *Wyoming* showing her port side. The casemate gunports have been plated over. Note the camouflage painting.   Photo June 1942

26

USS *Wyoming* in 1944 with her former three 12 in gun turrets removed. They were replaced by 5 in twin-turrets. Note the two-colour camouflage in accordance with Measure 22. The forward cage mast was later removed and replaced by a light pole mast. The side armour on the hull was also removed.

USS *Wyoming* in 1944 after the removal of her forward cage mast. Note the camouflage painting in accordance with Measure 22, i.e. the tint parallel closest to the deck line and the dark parallel next to the water line.   OUR NAVY Photo

BB 33 Arkansas

Radar Equipment

War Service:

			Forward	Aft
1942 Escort duty in the Atlantic		1942	SRa	SC
1943 Escort duty in the Atlantic and training ship		1944	SRa	SK
1944 Escort duty and shore bombardment off Normandy and the South of France		1945	SK, SRa	
1945 Iwo Jima, Okinawa				

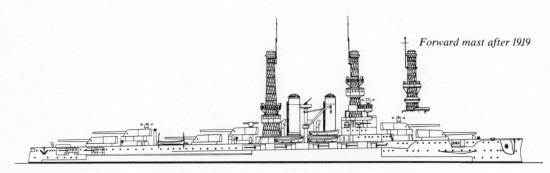

Forward mast after 1919

USS *Arkansas* in 1921. Range-finders are installed on three of her heavy gun turrets and on top of her bridge. Note the casemate guns still arranged on a single deck level.

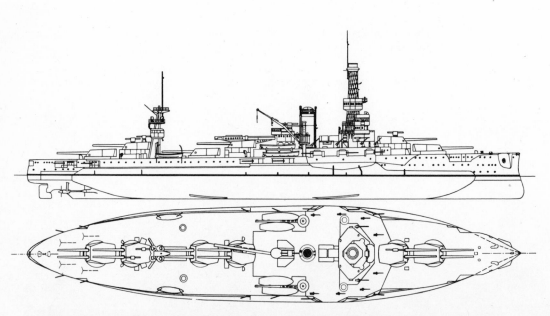

USS *Arkansas* in 1934. Bulges have been added. A catapult is mounted on the top of P-turret. Six of the 5 in L/51 casemate guns have been raised to the next deck. Her new superstructure overlaps her beam. Her X-turret has received a second range-finder.

BB 33 Arkansas

During the 1919 conversion all five aft casemate guns were removed including the fantail-mounted 5 in L/51 projecting over the transom. Again in 1925/27 *Arkansas* underwent conversion, the aft cagemast being replaced by a lower tripod and moved aft of turrets P and Q, and an aircraft catapult being installed on top of turret P. The forward 5 in guns were raised one deck and A.A. guns added. The sub-merged torpedo tubes were removed and aircraft handling gear installed on both sides of the funnel. In 1940/41 the elevation capability of the 12 in guns was increased by 15° to 30°. During 1942 all the medium guns were removed from the superstructure deck, the forward cagemast was replaced by a lower tripod, and the A.A. guns were given splinter-proof protection. In 1944 *Arkansas* received further modifications to her bridge and her aft mast.

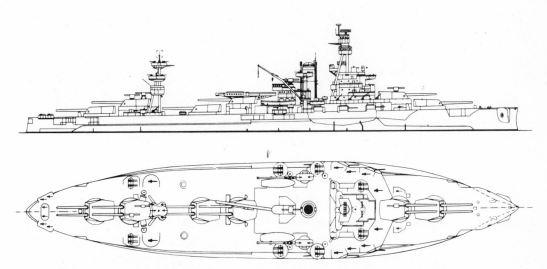

USS *Arkansas* in 1942. Her forward cage mast had been replaced by a tripod mast. All the remaining lower casemate guns had been removed. Sponson-mounted 40 mm A.A. guns were emplaced on deck and splinter-proof shields for her 3 in A.A. guns added. SRa and SC antennas were rigged on her forward and aft masts, respectively. Platforms carrying A.A. machine guns were placed around her aft mast and on either side of her funnel.

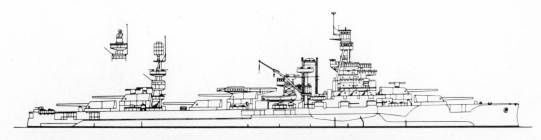

USS *Arkansas* in 1944. Her bridge superstructure and her aft mast were modified. Likewise, a SK radar screen was installed on her aft mast. Note the deck inclination toward her stern. The ship's aft mast was equipped with a Mk 37 fire control gear in 1945.

USS *Arkansas* firing a salute on her arrival at Kiel on July 5, 1930. Note the German naval flag on her mainmast.   Photo Schaefer

USS *Arkansas* in the early 1930's showing her midships section. There are two seaplanes on the catapult on top of turret 3. A 5 in L/51 casemate gun is fitted in a gunbay, whereas an open-mounted 5 in gun is installed abreast the bridge.   Photo Collection A. Barilli

Aerial view of USS *Arkansas* in the early 1930's. An awning has been installed abreast the bridge and B-turret. Note the range-finders on top of B- and X-turrets, also the crane and the seaplane catapult.

USS *Arkansas* during World War II with a small-sized pennant number on her bow, modified bridgework, and numerous A.A. gun stations.

USS *Arkansas* in 1945 riding high in the water. Note the traces of war actions. The SK radar screen has been moved from an aft to a forward position (SRa screen below it). Her aft mast and her bridge have been equipped with modern fire control gear and A.A. gun stations.

Photo J. A. Casoly. Collection Fr. Villi

New York Class

Following the *Wyoming* class it was planned to increase the main armament in the *New York* class by adding a seventh twin-turret, which in turn would have meant a further increase of length. This however was not acceptable. Rather more convenient alternatives were either five turrets of triple mounted 12 in (30.5 cm) guns or alternatively twin-turrets with 14 in (35.6 cm) guns instead of 12 in. The latter arrangement was finally adopted and the 14 in. (35.6 cm) caliber was made standard for a number of ships following the *New York* class.

Propulsion problems also arose with the *New York* class. Not fully acquainted with geared turbines, the builders refused to adopt specifications laid down by the Navy Department. Accordingly a reversion was made to reciprocating engines, then thought to be more economical.

In 1925/27 both ships underwent a period of extensive alterations similar to *Arkansas*. The original cagemasts—in this class very close to the former two funnels—were replaced by tripods. Both ships were converted to oil burning. The aircraft catapult was placed, at least for some time, next to the 'P' twin turret.

Both ships of this class were pioneers in shipborne radar. In December 1938 *New York* received an experimental radar antenna called XAF, installed above the bridge (as seen in the photograph), while *Texas* received a CXZ antenna. These ships and those of the classes that followed them were remarkable for the increased elevation given the guns in the main battery in the early 1940's. This increase, from 15° to 30°, gave greater range through permitting high trajectory firing. Its benefits were particularly recognised later in the war during shore bombardments.

During World War II the appearance of both ships remained little changed, apart from the installation of additional AA guns.

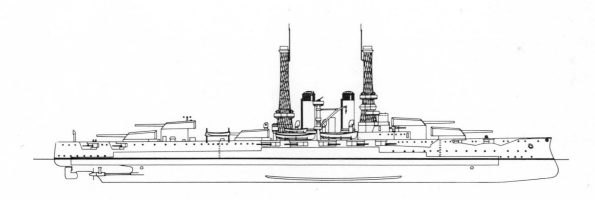

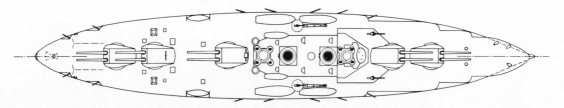

USS *New York* in 1918. The ship's heavy gun turrets housing the newly introduced 14 in guns differ in shape from those of former battleships. Her fantail-mounted 5 in casemate gun has already been removed. There are platform-mounted searchlights around her cage masts.

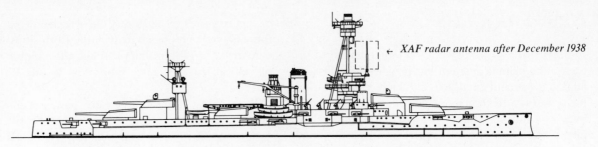

← *XAF radar antenna after December 1938*

USS *New York* in 1938. Her second funnel has been removed. Her cage masts have been replaced by tripod masts of different heights. Six of the 5 in L/51 guns have been raised to the next deck up, two of them occupying open mounts. This was done to protect them from spray and waves. All the 3 in A.A. guns are concentrated around the ship's bridge superstructure. An additional catapult was carried temporarily on the starboard side of Q-turret.

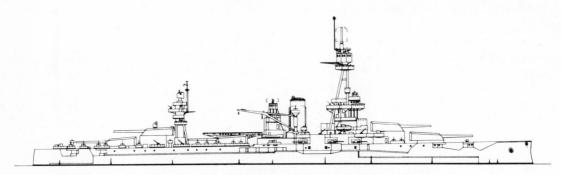

USS *New York* in 1945. Note gradual inclination of her deck towards her stern. The two lower 5 in L/51 guns have been removed. Light A.A. guns are massed on deck. SRa radar is installed abaft her funnel on her tower structure.

BB 34 New York

War Service:

1942 Escort duty in the Atlantic

1943 Escort duty in the Atlantic and training ship

1944 Escort duty in the Atlantic and shore bombardment off Normandy and the South of France.

1945 Joined the Pacific Fleet after overhaul: Iwo Jima, Okinawa

Radar Equipment

	Forward	Aft
1938	XAF	
1942	SC, SRa	SRa
1944	SRa	SRa
1945	SK	

BB 34 New York

In 1925 *New York* was converted in a similar way to other battleships built before or during World War I. The second funnel was removed and both cagemasts replaced by tripods, the mainmast being moved to a position aft of turret Q. One catapult was installed on turret Q, and the medium armament regrouped as in *Arkansas*. In 1940/41 the elevation of the 12 in guns was increased to 30°, and the aft 5 in casemate guns were removed. The 3 in A.A. guns were increased to a total of ten and received splinter-proof protection, while more 20 mm and 40 mm were added.

Undamaged after the outbreak of hostilities while she was in the Atlantic, *New York* appearance did not change much during the war except for the addition of A.A. guns and electronic installations. *New York* was the first U.S. battleship to receive an experimental radar system. Fitted in December 1938 it had a bridge-mounted XAF antenna.

Side view of USS *New York* in the early 1930's. Note three aircraft placed on one catapult, and the ship's extremely short quarterdeck.   Collection A. Fraccaroli

Aerial view of USS *New York* in the mid-1930's. The forward casemate guns have been removed. There is a single 5 in gun in an open mount abreast the bridge superstructure and an additional 3 in A.A. gun behind the 5 in gun mount. Note the searchlights on the aft mast platform.

The bridge superstructure of USS *New York* in 1939 during tests with the first operational shipboard radar, designated XAF. Note the upper bridge and the conning tower below. The 5 in L/51 gun next to the bridge is placed in an open mount.   Photo ''USNI Proceedings''

USS *New York* during the war, probably in 1944, with her camouflage painting according to Measure 22 "graded system" a small-sized pennant number on her bow, and numerous A.A. gun stations. The life rafts are attached to the sides of the heavy gun turrets. 20 mm A.A. guns are mounted on platforms atop the masts. SRa radar screens are carried on her foremast and abaft the funnel.

USS *New York* in 1945 returning from the theatre of war to the US West Coast. Note her hull damaged below A-turret above the water line. The SG, SK, and SRa radar antennas are carried on her foremasts. Also note the 20 mm A.A. gun stations on both her masts. Battle scores have been painted on the side of her bridge. The pipes visible along her hull line may be fuel pipelines. New models of fire control equipment are installed atop the bridge and on the slightly modified aft mast. Photo J. A. Casoly, Collection Fr. Villi

BB 35 Texas

Radar Equipment

War Service:

		Forward	Aft
1942 Escort duty in the Atlantic and off North Africa	1938	CXZ	
1943 Escort duty in the Atlantic and gunnery train- ing ship on the East Coast	1942	SRa	SRa
	1943	SRa	SC, SRa
1945 Iwo Jima, Okinawa, and period in dock	1948	SRa	SK, SRa

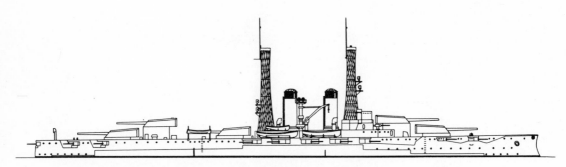

USS *Texas* in 1930. She is still carrying her forward and fantail-mounted casemate guns. Her cage masts do not carry distinct platforms.

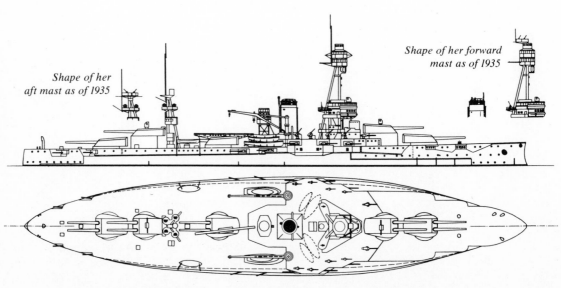

Shape of her aft mast as of 1935

Shape of her forward mast as of 1935

USS Texas *in 1930. At this time she resembled USS* New York *in appearance.*

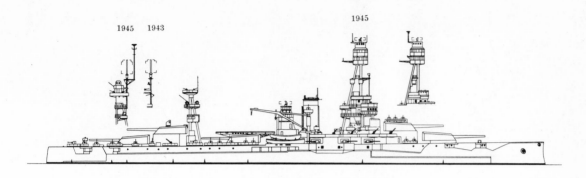

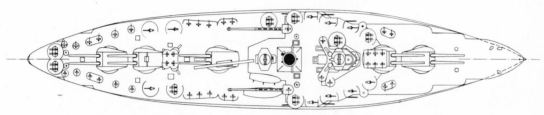

USS *Texas* in 1942. SRa radar antenna are installed on her fore mast and abaft her funnel on the tower structure. 20 mm A.A. guns are mounted on platforms on top of her B-turret. Her deck plan is "asymmetrical". Her port side shows the light A.A. battery after the regrouping done in 1945.

Also shown are the ways her aft mast was modified as of 1945 and 1943 (carrying a SK radar antenna.)

BB 35 Texas

Modifications to *Texas* were similar to those made to *New York*. In December 1938 the experimental radar antenna CXZ was installed on the bridge. During the war a group of six 20 mm A.A. guns were mounted on top of turret B, distinguishing this battleship from her sistership *New York*. The aft mast was modified in 1944, and in 1945 the light A.A. gun battery regrouped (see deck plan).

USS *Texas* on trial runs at 15 knots. Her aft mast has not yet been given its "cork." Note the out-dated types of air intakes. The date is October 1913.

USS *Texas* in about 1935. Her appearance has completely changed since her completion. The forward casemate gunports have been plated over. The midships 5 in L/51 guns have been housed in gunbays. Range-finders can now be seen on the B and X-turrets as well as on top of the bridge.

The forward section of USS *Texas*, probably in 1943. A small-sized pennant number is painted on her bow above the water line. Note the SC radar screen placed above the SRa antenna. The casemate guns are swung out.

An instructive aerial view of USS *Texas* as she appeared in April 1944. The camouflage painting is in accordance with Measure 22. Numerous 40 mm and 20 mm A.A. gun stations have been installed, even atop the B and X-turrets. The casemate guns are swung out. Note that the radar screen on her aft mast is hardly visible.

USS *Texas* returning from the theatre of war to the US West Coast in 1945. The crew are manning the rails. The ship is still carrying two SRa screens in addition to one SK antenna on the aft mast.   Photo J. A. Casoly, Collection Fr. Villi

USS *Texas* as a memorial ship near Houston after World War II. Note the two SRa's and the SK screens still mounted on her masts.   Photo Texas Highway Dept.

Nevada Class

The design of these ships marked a new era in naval construction. During the 1912 firing practice exercises it was realised that vital parts of the ship needed better protection, including protecting the underwater area of the hull against torpedoes. The way this had been done in the past by armored protection all over the ship was incompatible with the new requirements as it would have meant an unwarranted increase of weight from armor plating.

Finally both ships of this class were conceived and built with completely new features embodying the "all-or-nothing" concept. This meant adequate armored protection for the vital parts of the ship leaving the rest more or less unprotected.

The 14 in main battery of the *Nevada* received a new mounting of triple-turrets, enabling the construction to follow the successful arrangement of the past by placing two turrets of the main battery forward and two aft. The lower turrets 'A' and 'Y' were in triple mounts and the turrets 'B' and 'X' in twin mounts. This arrangement and the grouping of the main batteries provided the same fire power as the *New York* class with one turret less.

The *Nevada* class embodied other features differing from its forerunners. The "flush-deck" was not used. *Nevada's* forecastle deck was extended over 3/5ths of the ship's length, the remainder being lowered by one deck level. This subsequently enabled the constructors, during the first large-scale modernization in the mid-1920's, to raise the secondary battery—placed in casemates—by one deck in order to give it 'drier' working conditions. As in previous classes a seaplane catapult was installed on a turret of the main battery—here on turret X—while a second catapult was added on the fantail deck. Both ships received oil burning boilers when they were built.

During the Japanese attack on Pearl Harbor *Nevada* and *Oklahoma* were extensively damaged. *Oklahoma* was found to be beyond repair and not worth rebuilding. *Nevada* was luckier. After 12 months of complete rebuilding she rejoined the fleet, with her pre-war silhouette changed. Her new inclined funnel cap was the most distinctive outward feature of the reconstruction.

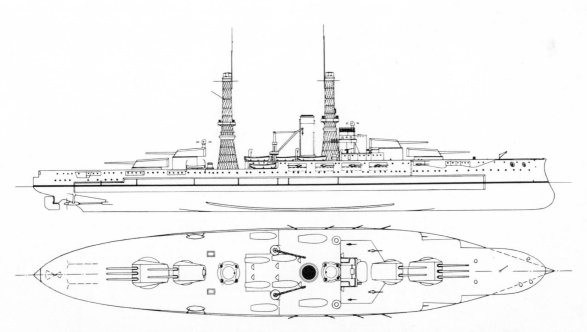

USS *Nevada* in 1920. Four turret ships have made a comeback. There is only one funnel left. Her forecastle deck is extended, her quarterdeck is one deck lower. Her stepped stern section formerly bore a casemate gun.

BB 36 Nevada

War Service:

1942 Covering force duty in the North Atlantic, Repairs; escort duty in the Atlantic and off North Africa

1943 Escort duty in the Atlantic

1944 Escort duty in the Atlantic and off the South of France

1945 Iwo Jima, Okinawa, and training at Leyte

Radar Equipment

	Forward	Aft
1942	SRa	SRa
1943	SK, SRa	SRa
1945	SK, SRa	SRa

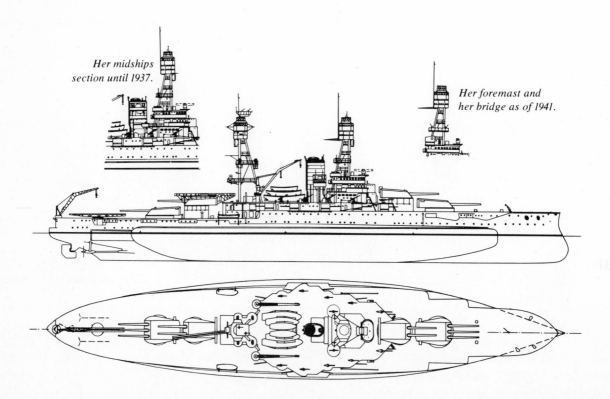

Her midships section until 1937.

Her foremast and her bridge as of 1941.

USS *Nevada* in 1938. Her long quarterdeck permitted the installation of a catapult on the fantail. Her aft mast has been replaced by a huge tripod structure and her bridge reconstructed. The 5 in casemate guns have been raised a deck. Note the concentrated stowage of the ship's boats. Hull bulges added.

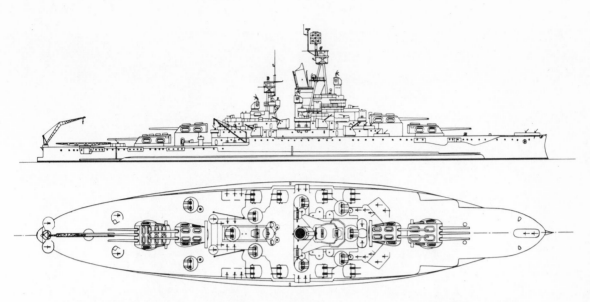

USS *Nevada* in 1945. Total reconstruction completely changed her appearance. She now has a slanted funnel cap and a SK radar screen on her foremast. Both her bow and her stern carry 20 mm A.A. guns. The life rafts are stowed on the sides of her 14 in gun turrets. Her 5 in L/38 twin-turrets are arranged in a similar way as on board the *Tennessee*.

BB 36 Nevada

During the 1927/29 conversion both cagemasts were replaced by tripods, the bridge was modified, the 5 in guns were raised one deck and the torpedo tubes removed. Two catapults were installed on turret X and on the quarter deck. The bulges added at this time reduced the speed of the ship. In 1935/36 the height of the funnel was increased. Whereas ships of the previous two classes had flush-decks the main decks of *Nevada* and *Oklahoma* covered only a little more than half of the ship's length. The lower quarter deck was therefore "wet" in heavy seas. *Nevada* was

damaged at Pearl Harbor, but the captain succeeded in beaching her. She was then completely rebuilt with a new re-arranged superstructure to permit improved firing arcs for her A.A. guns; a higher bridge linked with the funnel; and a high funnel cap inclined aft. Other changes included the removal of all medium guns and of the catapult previously placed on turret X plus its handling gear. After this conversion *Nevada* rejoined the fleet looking considerably changed. The eight new 5 in gun twin-mounts were controlled by four MK 37 fire control systems and their associated radars. In addition forty-eight 40 mm and twenty-seven 20 mm A.A. guns were installed, though their numbers changed later in the war.

Impressive picture taken of USS *Nevada* running at high speed, with turrets A, B, and Y swung out. There is a total of three aircraft on both of her catapults. She is equipped with huge tripod masts. Her long forecastle ends at the aircraft crane. Her pennant number "36" shows on the roof of B-turret. She is carrying a large number of boats.

USS *Nevada*, probably in the middle of the 1930's. Note that the forward and aft casemate guns have already been removed whereas the midships casemate guns have been mounted on the upperdeck level. One of the hawseholes is empty. Due to the presence of a second battleship behind, possibly the USS *Oklahoma*, the aft part silhouette of USS *Nevada* is not clearly visible.   Collection S. Breyer

USS *Nevada* during World War II, immediately after her reconstruction. Note the unique funnel cap, and the four MK 37 gunnery control equipments on top of the bridge, abreast the funnel, and directly abaft the short aft tripod. The fire control radar is carried atop the Mk 37s.   Photo December 1942

Oblique view of USS *Nevada* after her reconstruction. Note the break in her quarterdeck and the small-sized pennant number aft, close to the 40 mm A.A. gun station. Two SRa radar antennas are installed. The midships catwalk overlaps the deck side. The aft aircraft crane has been mounted on the fantail.   Photo December 1942

USS *Nevada* in 1944 during the bombardment of Cherbourg. She is still carrying two SRa radar antennas, but has been rigged with an additional SK antenna on her foremast. The 5 in guns are swung out and elevated against enemy aircraft.   Collection Barilli

USS *Nevada* with camouflage painting according to Measure 22. Note the elongated counter-sunk 20 mm A.A. gun stations on her forecastle. Her A.A. guns are massed midships. The SK and SRa antennas are visible on her foremast. OUR NAVY Photo

BB 37 Oklahoma

War Service:
1941 Sunk in Pearl Harbor

Radar Equipment

No radar antennae were installed on this ship before Pearl Harbor.

Pre-war modifications of the *Oklahoma* were similar to those made to her sister *Nevada*. *Oklahoma* was torpedoed at Pearl Harbor, and capsized in shallow water. Righted and refloated in 1944, it was decided after survey that she was not worth rebuilding.* The recovered barrels of her main battery were later used on BB 38 *Pennsylvania*. While on tow from Pearl Harbor to the West Coast for scrap, *Okklahoma* broke her tow and foundered in the Pacific on May 17, 1947.

* Detailed illustrated report on recovery of this ship in "U.S. Naval Institute Proceedings", December 1975.

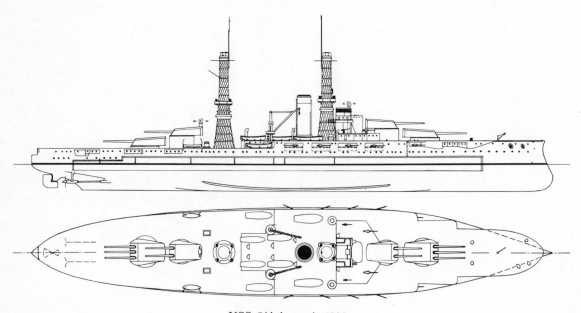

USS *Oklahoma* in 1920

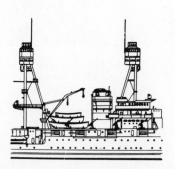

USS *Oklahoma* in 1930 showing her midship section

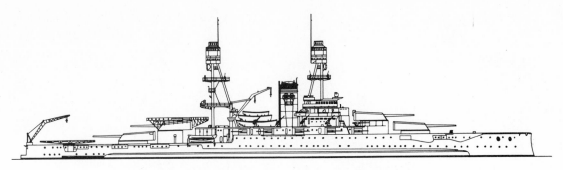

USS *Oklahoma* in 1936. Note the supporting structure of the catapult on top of X-turret.

USS *Oklahoma* two years after her completion. Since all other gunports are closed, only the two forward 5 in L/51 casemate guns can be seen. A total of eight searchlights are mounted.
Photo December 1918

USS *Oklahoma* anchoring off the Cuban coast in January 1920. Her forward casemate guns
have been removed. Note the gunport blinds opened for the occasion. The ramp for a light
airplane can be seen on B-turret.   Photo January 1920

USS *Oklahoma* in the years shortly before World War II. Note the similar arrangement of
both her mast platforms.   Collection A. Fraccaroli

USS *Oklahoma* during gun drill in the 1930's. Note the muzzle covers on the gun barrels of A-turret. All her guns are swung out.

Pennsylvania Class

This class of battleships incorporated further improvements over its predecessors. Geared turbine engines were at last adopted. 14 in caliber guns were retained for the main battery, but the number of them was increased by two by making all four turrets triple ones. This was in response to designs adopted by the Japanese for their battleships *Fuso* and *Yamashiro*, then under construction. Again the United States preferred to follow the example of other seapowers, rather than to initiate innovations.

The modernisation of the *Pennsylvania* class after World War I and again between 1928 and 1931 was similar to changes made to the *Nevada* class. Additionally the funnel heights of the *Pennsylvania* ships were increased slightly before World War II. During the war the catapults on the X turret were removed and replaced by three splinter-proof protected mounts for 20 mm A.A. guns. The B turret also received a similar mounting.

Arizona's magazines exploded after she was torpedoed and bombed and she was found to be past repair. Her wreck was not raised. *Pennsylvania* received one bomb hit only and re-joined the fleet six months later.

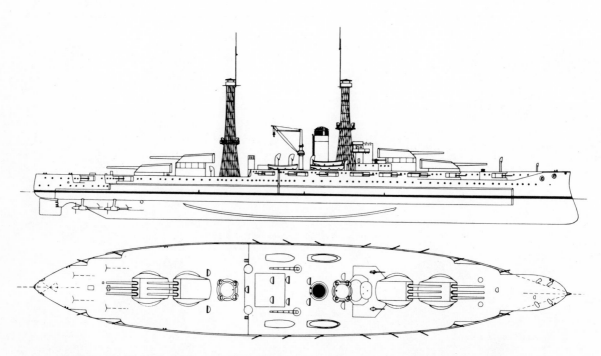

USS *Pennsylvania* in 1917, presenting a "normal" stern section. She is similar in appearance to the ships of the *Nevada* class. All her heavy guns are mounted in triple-turrets. Note the obsolete shape of the ventilator coamings.

BB 38 Pennsylvania

War Service:

1942: Damage sustained at Pearl Harbor repaired. Covering force duty off the West Coast and Hawaii. Dockyard overhaul.

1943 Period in dock. Covering force duty off the West Coast and Attu. Repairs. Kiska. Work up period off Hawaii, Makin.

1944 Kwajalein Majuro (Marshall Islands), Eniwetok. Covering Force duty and training in South West Pacific, Saipan, Guam, Southern Palau Islands, Leyte, Surigao Strait.

1945 Lingayen. Period in dock. Work up off the West Coast. Wake, Okinawa. Damage repaired.

Radar Equipment

	Forward	*Aft*
1941	CXAM	
1943	SRa	SRa, CXAM
1945	SK-2	SP

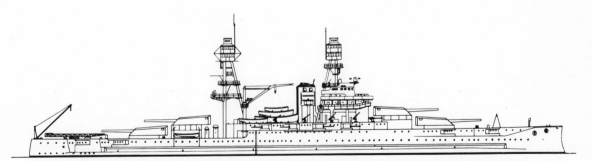

USS *Pennsylvania* in 1931. Her midships casemate guns have been raised to a higher deck while her fore and aft casemate guns have been removed and all gunports plated over. Her cage masts have been replaced by heavy tripod masts. Her armament has been reinforced by A.A. guns, a catapult placed on the fantail, and her boat hoists moved to new positions.

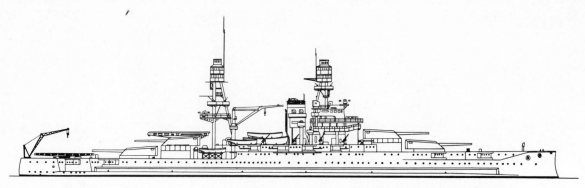

USS *Pennsylvania* in 1939. A catapult has been installed on top of X-turret, while the ship's boats are placed abreast her aft mast. The height of her funnel has been increased.

Her bridge and aft superstructure after 1945.

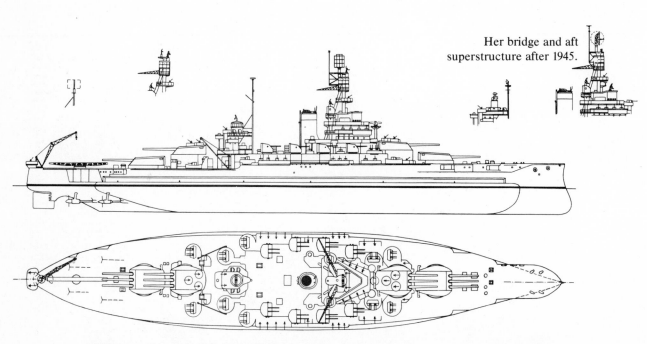

USS *Pennsylvania* in 1943. Her aft tripod mast has been replaced by a tower superstructure. 20 mm A.A. gun platform mounts have been installed atop her B- and X-turret and her 5 in L/38 mounts arranged on a single deck level. The ship was equipped with only two Mk 37 fire controls. All bull's eyes were plated over.

The radar equipment carried as of summer 1943: one CXAM antenna on her aft pole mast, two platform-mounted SRa screens on her fore mast.

BB 38 Pennsylvania

This ship received extensive modifications similar to *Nevada* after World War I and again in the early 1930's. *Pennsylvania* was in dry dock at Pearl Harbor on December 7th 1941, and did not escape serious damage. At that time she already carried the CXAM radar aerial on her forward tripod mast.

In 1942/43 all her old medium guns were removed and replaced by eight radar-controlled 5 in L/38 twin mounts, placed on the superstructure deck. Only two Mk 37 radar directed fire control equipments were installed. The light A.A. battery received forty 40 mm and fifty 20 mm guns, but these numbers were changed again later in the war. The catapult on turret X with its aircraft handling gear was removed, and the heavy aft tripod mast was replaced by a light pole mast carrying the CXAM antenna that had formerly been fitted on the forward tripod mast. All the portholes in the hull were plated over.

Pennsylvania received considerable damage from a Japanese aircraft torpedo attack in August 1945, and her career ended as a target ship for nuclear bomb tests in 1946. Pre-war modifications to *Arizona* were similar to those made to her sister ship *Pennsylvania*, except that the height of the funnel was not increased.

USS *Pennsylvania* in the early 1920's. She still has her two cage masts. Note her wooden deck and the narrow space between the 14 in gun barrels.

USS *Pennsylvania* in the 1930's. Her aft cage mast has been replaced by a tripod mast. There are chine-type frames on the fore part of her hull.

USS *Pennsylvania* immediately after her wartime reconstruction in February 1943. All portholes have been plated over. In this photograph the enlarged bridge gives a false impression of her funnel having been removed. She carries two Mk 37 fire control equipments with their associated radars.
Photo February 1943

A side view of USS *Pennsylvania*. Note the range-finder in front of her bridge. All 5 in L/38 twin-mounts are placed on the same deck whereas the 20 mm gun platforms are installed beside her bridge, atop B- and X-turret, and along the deck edge.   Photo February 1943

Oblique view of USS *Pennsylvania* from astern. Note the barrels of Y-turret closed by muzzle covers and the derricks placed abreast the aft 14 in gun turret. The latter carries the SRa antenna. The CXAM antenna is installed on the ship's pole mast. Also note the catapult with the fantail-sited aircraft handling crane and the 20 mm A.A. gun station.

Photo February 1943

One of the best known and most impressive photographs showing US warships in "line ahead": the *Pennsylvania* with her 5 in guns swung out leads the USS *Colorado* (BB 45), USS *Louisville* (CA 28), USS *Portland* (CA 33), and USS *Columbia* (CL 56) in a battle line entering the Lingayen Gulf preceding the landings on Luzon. Photo January 1945

USS *Pennsylvania*, a photograph probably taken after World War II. Two of the 5 in twin-mounts on her port side and some of the 40 mm four-barrelled A.A. guns have been removed. The SK-2 radar is installed atop her foremast with the platform-mounted 20 mm A.A. guns placed below. Note the covered cockpits of the shipborne aircraft.

BB 39 Arizona

Arizona was sunk at Pearl Harbor on December 7, 1941 and became a national symbol for all the losses of ships and men in that attack. A shrine was later erected above her. Two of her 14 in gun turrets were recovered and installed as coastal defence artillery on the island, in which role they were manned by army personnel.

War Service:
1941 Sunk at Pearl Harbor

Radar Equipment

Up to the time of Pearl Harbor no radar had been fitted to *Arizona*.

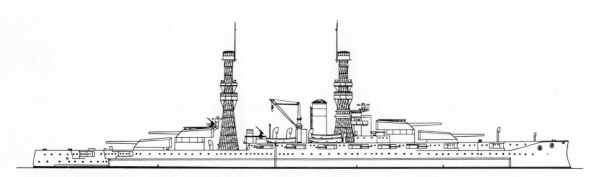

USS *Arizona* in 1921. Both her bow and stern casemate guns have already been removed. Her armament was reinforced by A.A. guns.

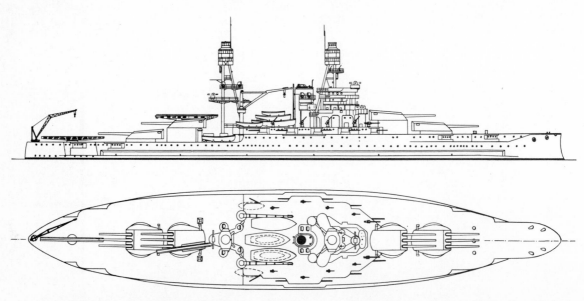

USS *Arizona* in 1936. Her remaining casemate guns had been raised to the next deck, but there were still two more of them than on board the *Pennsylvania*. A catapult was mounted on top of her X-turret.

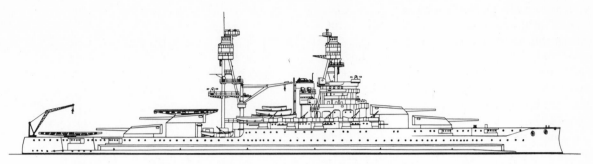

USS *Arizona* in 1941. There are hardly any changes in her appearance as compared to 1936. She now carries platform-mounted machine guns on her masts. The number of 5 in A.A. guns has been increased. They all received splinter-proof shields.

USS *Arizona* in the 1930's. She was sunk at Pearl Harbor on December 7, 1941. Note the two aircraft handling cranes abreast her aft tripod mast mounted high for the purpose of lifting seaplanes onto the X-turret catapult. Also note the pointed shape of the ship's stern.

New Mexico Class

In general this class followed similar lines to the *Pennsylvanias* though with further improvements. The same arrangement of the main battery was employed, but the 14 in guns were of an improved design. During construction some of the 5 in casemate guns were raised to a higher deck level to keep them dry in heavy seas. An innovation was the clipper bow given to both this and subsequent classes of battleships, excepting only the *North Carolina* and the *South Dakota*.

Originally the *New Mexicos* were fitted with turbo-electric drive, which was replaced by geared turbines during modernisation in 1930-34.

Contrary to the normal practice of building two ships in each class, the U.S. Navy ordered three *New Mexicos*. The third—*Idaho*—received its appropriation from Congress after the sale of the old battleships *Mississippi* (BB 23) and *Idaho* (BB 24) to Greece. As a result of the 1930-34 rebuilding, the *New Mexicos* remained the most modern battleships in the U.S. Navy until the advent of the *North Carolina* class.

As none of the three were at Pearl Harbor at the end of 1941, their appearance was not changed by repair or rebuilding as happened to ships that were damaged. Only more A.A. armament and fire control equipment were added, although a planned replacement of the older 5 in L/25 AA guns by sixteen 5 in L/38s had still not been carried out when the war ended.

After the war one of the class—*Mississippi*—served as an experimental gunnery training ship and later as a guided missile test ship.

USS *Arizona* in the 1930's. Note the similarity of her fore and aft tripod masts.

OUR NAVY Photo

BB 40 New Mexico

Radar Equipment

War Service:

1942 Covering Force duty off West Coast: Training. Covering Force and Escort duty South West Pacific.
1943 Covering Force duty South Pacific, Attu, Aleutians. Period in dock, Makin.
1944 Kwajalein Majuro, Kavieng. Training. Saipan, Guam. Period in dock.
1945 Repairs. Occupation of Japan.

	Forward	*Aft*
1942	SRa	SRa
1944	SK, SRa	SRa

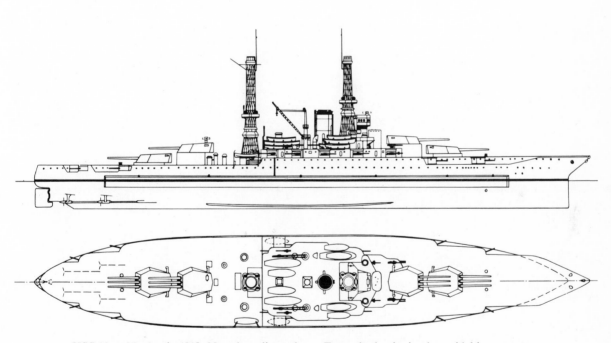

USS *New Mexico* in 1918. Note her clipper bow. From the beginning her midship casemate guns were emplaced one deck higher than those on other battleships. She carried only a few A.A. guns.

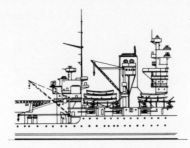

The midship section of USS *New Mexico* in 1936. Her former cage masts have been replaced by tower superstructures. The number of A.A. guns has been increased. She has a catapult on X-turret (see plan of the *Mississippi* in 1936).

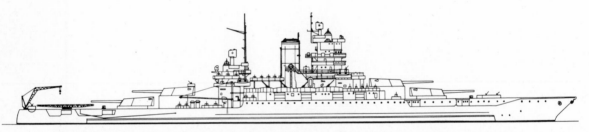

USS *New Mexico* in 1942. All casemate guns and the catapult once installed on top of X-turret have been removed. She is equipped with improved fire control gear. All A.A. guns are protected by splinter-proof shields. A "flying platform" for her 20 mm A.A. guns has been erected abaft her funnel.

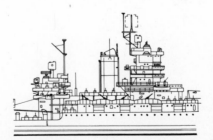

USS *New Mexico* in 1945. The drawing shows her midship section. SK radar has been installed on her fore mast top, and the SRa screen can be seen on her aft tower. Her funnel has received a cap. The 20 mm A.A. guns have been regrouped.

BB 40 New Mexico

During the modernisation of 1930-34 both cagemasts were replaced by tower superstructures and the aft tower was given a pole topmast. The forward tower with a short tubular topmast incorporated the bridge. Two of the 5 in L/51 guns mounted aft on the upper deck were removed and so were the submerged torpedo tubes. The A.A. guns received fire control gear. Catapults were installed on turret X and on the quarter deck together with cranes for handling aircraft.

As they were stationed in the Atlantic at the time the Japanese attacked Pearl Harbor, all three ships of this class avoided damage then. In 1942 all of the 5 in L/51 guns and the catapult on turret X plus its han-

dling gear were removed. Two "flying platforms" with six 20 mm A.A. guns each were installed and sited abreast the funnel (to port and starboard). This arrangement was carried by *New Mexico* until about 1944. The proposed replacement of the 5 in L/25 guns by L/38's in twin-mounts was abandoned at the end of the war.

New Mexico was twice hit by Kamikazes, in January 1945 and August 1945. (Kamikazes were Japanese aircraft loaded with explosives, and guided onto their target by suicide pilots. This desperate weapon was deployed by the Japanese in the last phase of the war. More than 160 U.S. ships were hit by Kamikazes, but no capital ships were lost as a result.)

USS *New Mexico* in 1940. Note the casemate gun recesses with their gunports plated over.

Aerial view of USS *New Mexico* in the 1930's. Note her tower bridge superstructure, her oval citadel, and her stepped hull shape with its vertical armour plating. A canvas awning covers the fantail. Also note the recesses where the casemate guns were formerly mounted.

USS *New Mexico* after her reconstruction during World War II. All casemate guns have been removed. Her A.A. guns are concealed by splinter-proof covers. Note the elevated "flying platforms" on either side abaft her funnel. Each platform carries six 20 mm A.A. guns.

USS *New Mexico* in three-colour camouflage according to Measure 32. There is a SK radar screen on her foremast whereas a SRa antenna is mounted on her bridge superstructure, and another SRa aerial on her aft tower superstructure. Note her sharply contoured clipper bow and her bow hawsepipe without an anchor.

BB 41 Mississippi

War Service:
1942 Escort Duty West Coast. Training ship West Coast and Hawaii. Covering Force Duty South West Pacific.
1943 Covering Force Duty South West Pacific. Attu. Period in dock. Makin.
1944 Kwajelein Majuro, Kavieng. Period in dock. Southern Palau Islands, Leyte, Surigao Straits, Mindoro.
1945 Lingayen. Repairs. Okinawa. Period in dock. Training Exercises. Occupation of Japan.

Radar Equipment:

	Forward	Aft
1944	SRa	SK, SRa
1949	?	SPS 8A
1954	SPS 6	SPS 8A
1956	SPS 6	SPS 8B

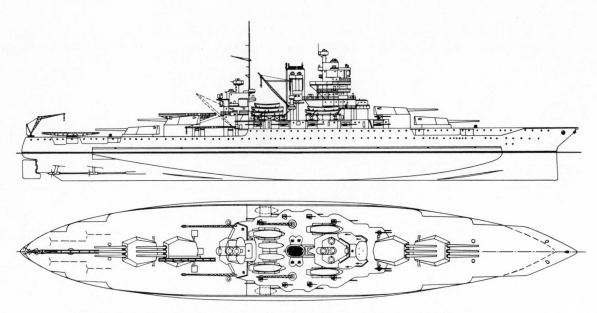

USS *Mississippi* in 1936. Her former bow and stern casemate guns have been removed. There was no difference between her appearance and that of *New Mexico* at this time. Note the new shape of her 14 in gun turrets.

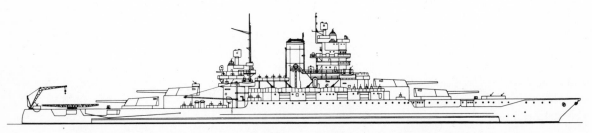

USS *Mississippi* in 1942. Except for the "flying platform" for A.A. guns abaft her funnel she is similar in appearance to the *New Mexico*. Such a "flying platform" may never have been fitted to the *Mississippi*.

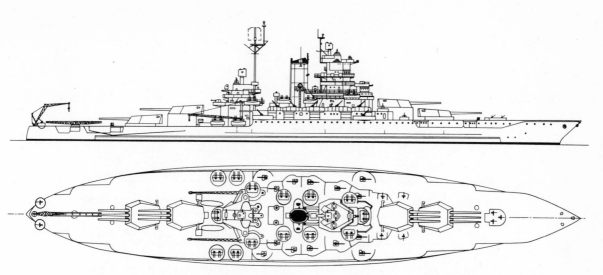

USS *Mississippi* in 1945. A SK radar is rigged on her aft mast. Additional 5 in L/25 and 40 mm A.A. guns have been mounted. The platform-mounted 20 mm A.A. guns have been removed from X-turret. Her funnel has a slanted cap.

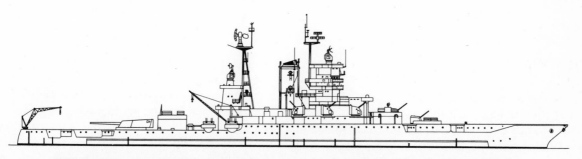

USS *Mississippi* in 1949. She has been converted into a gunnery experimental ship. Only her aftermost 14 in gun turret is left. Note the various 5 in gun single- and twin-mounts. Her forward top bears a radar screen. Her aft tripod mast shows an early model of the SPS 8A radar antenna. The four aft 40 mm gun mounts belonging to her former wartime A.A. armament and the aft crane of her former aircraft handling equipment are still in place.

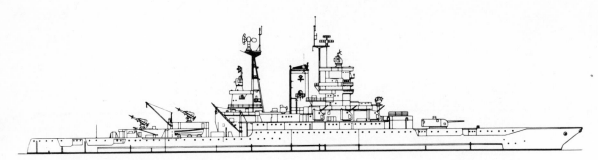

USS *Mississippi* in 1955. In place of her obsolete heavy gun turret barbette in the A turret position a new and fully automatic 6 in L/47 A.A. gun twin-turret has been mounted. This 6 in twin-turret type was originally fitted on the two A.A. cruisers of the *Worcester* class. The type of radar shown in this plan of 1955 may not be correct—see the photographs on the following pages showing radar equipment carried in other years. Instead of the aft heavy gun barbettes two experimental launchers of the "Terrier" guided missile system with magazines have been installed.

BB 41 Mississippi

Mississippi's pre-war modifications were similar to those made to her sister ship, *New Mexico*. At the time America entered the war she was stationed in the Atlantic. Around 1943 a slanted funnel cap was fitted. Other wartime modifications followed those made to *New Mexico*, except that no photographs of the ship show the 'flying platform' for 20 mm A.A. guns, which other sources indicate was fitted but soon after removed during 1942. In 1944 six 5 in L/25 A.A. guns were added.

Mississippi was twice hit by Kamikazes (in January 1945 and June 1945) and slightly damaged.

Soon after the war (February 1946) work was started on converting *Mississippi* into a gunnery test ship (see drawings and photographs), reclassified as AG 128. After completion she replaced AG 17 *Wyoming*. *Mississippi* underwent a second conversion in 1952 to serve as a guided missile test ship for the "Terrier" system, besides being a test ship for gunnery, fire control systems and radar equipment. Like *Wyoming* she was "unsymmetrical" in appearance since the siting of the armament on one side was different to that on the other.

USS *Mississippi* in the 1920s. Her aft and forward casemate guns have already been removed. Range-finders are installed on top of her bridge and her X-turret.

USS *Mississippi* in the 1930s. The cage masts have already been removed and replaced by a tower bridge in the forward position and a control tower in the aft position. Note the improved range-finder equipment. Aircraft are carried on both catapults.

A Navy Model of USS *Mississippi* as she appeared after her reconstruction in the 1930s (midships section).

USS *Mississippi* in the early months of 1942 before the casemate guns were removed. Her camouflage painting corresponds to Measure 22. Her A.A. guns are protected by splinter-proof covers. Her funnel is still without a cap.   Collection A. Barilli

Aerial view of USS *Mississippi*, probably in 1944. She now has a funnel cap, numerous A.A. gun stations, and SK radar antenna on her aft mast. There is no "flying platform" for A.A. guns abaft the funnel.

USS *Mississippi* following her conversion into a gunnery experimental ship. Her small-sized pennant number is painted on her bow. For her silhouette see the drawing on p. 81. The aft 14 in gun turret is still fitted. Three 5 in L/38 twin-mounts are positioned on her starboard side. Note the early model of the SPS 8A air search antenna. The Mk 37 fire control gear is carried on the bridge superstructure.   Collection G. Albrecht

USS *Mississippi* after 1952—see also the drawing on p. 82. The crane has been removed and two Terrier launchers have been installed aft. She carries a SPS 6 radar antenna on her foremast, MK 56 fire control gear in front of the bridge, and an early model of the Mk 68 fire control gear on top of the bridge. A 6 in L/47 twin-turret is placed in front of the barbette of former B-turret and two 5 in L/54 turrets are on her port side. A large-sized pennant number is painted on her bow.   Collection F. Villi

USS *Mississippi* in 1956. She carries two experimental Terrier launchers aft. A Mk 37 fire control gear with an additional radar screen for guided missile control above it is installed on the aft tower superstructure. (The latter radar screen type was later fitted to USS *Boston* (CAG 1) during her first months of service as a Guided Missile Cruiser.) A SPS 6 radar antenna is carried on the foremast. On top of the bridge below it is the Mk 68 fire control gear introduced at that time for the new 5 in L/54 DP guns. The rarely installed SPS 8B radar antenna is carried on her aft mast. Note also a small-sized TACAN aircraft navigation aid on her aft mast top.   Collection A. Fraccaroli

One of the last photographs of USS *Mississippi* before her decommissioning. Note the SPS 8B antenna atop her aft mast. Photo April 1956, W. H. Davis. Collection G. Albrecht

BB 42 Idaho

War Service:
1942 Covering Force duties West Coast and Hawaii.
1943 Work up period. Covering Force duties in the Aleutians, Attu, Kiska. Dockyard repairs. Makin.
1944 Kwajalein Majuro. Work up period. Saipan, Guam, Southern Palau islands. Dockyard repairs.
1945 Work up period. Iwo Jima, Okinawa. Occupation of Japan.

Radar Equipment

	Forward	Aft
1942	SRa	SRa
1944	SK	SRa

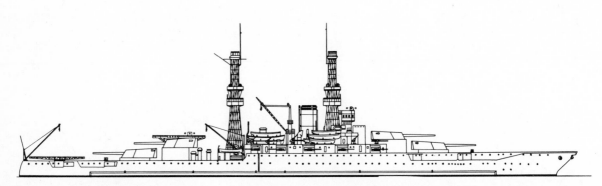

USS *Idaho* shown in the first years of her commissioning. Her forward and aft casemate guns have already been removed. The catapults and the aircraft handling crane had not yet been installed. In 1936 she resembled the *New Mexico* and the *Mississippi*.

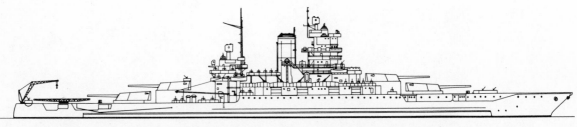

USS *Idaho* in 1942. She resembles the *New Mexico* and the *Mississippi* in appearance. The "flying platform" for the 20 mm A.A. guns has not been erected yet.

USS *Idaho* in 1945. The ship's forward section shows the stepped shape of her side armour. She carries a SK radar screen on her fore mast top. Her 20 mm A.A. guns have been placed close to the fore mast.

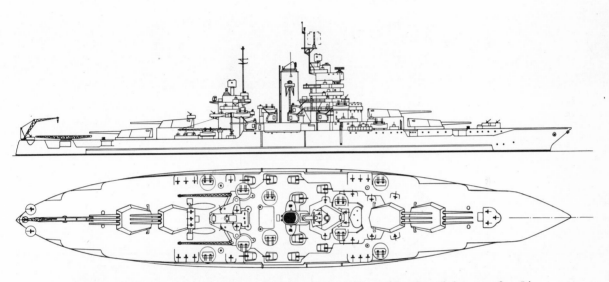

USS *Idaho* in 1945 with a sharply slanted funnel cap. Abreast her funnel there are five 5 in L/38 single-mounts on either side, placed on different deck levels. A 20 mm gun platform is on top of Z-turret. Besides the SK radar the *Idaho* is equipped with a SRa screen on her foretop. Her funnel is shown at its full height.

BB 42 Idaho

Idaho's pre-war modifications were similar to *New Mexico's*. Along with her sister ships she was on the 'Atlantic Neutrality Patrol' in 1941. Wartime changes were again no greater than those made to *New Mexico* and there is no evidence that a 'flying platform' for A.A. guns was ever installed. In 1943 all her old 5 in A.A. guns were replaced by newer 5 in L/38 guns in single mounts—a unique arrangement for a battleship. Her funnel was given a slanted cap. *Idaho* was hit by a torpedo from an aircraft in April 1945.

USS *Idaho* before World War II with USS *New Mexico* in the background. Note the searchlights on the platforms beside the funnel.   Collection A. Fraccaroli

USS *Idaho* after her first wartime modification. She looks similar to the *Mississippi*, but her casemate guns have been removed.   Photo December 1942

USS *Idaho* after her modification in 1943. She carries her SK radar antenna on the foremast. Her SRa antenna is mounted on top of her aft tower superstructure. Note the 5 in single gun mount beside the funnel.

USS *Idaho* in 1943 after her last modifications. Note the enlarged structure carrying the 5 in L/38 single-mounts. The SRa radar antenna is mounted above the bridge. She has a very narrow base for her stabilized range-finders. Note the unusual funnel cap.

Collection A. Fraccaroli

Tennessee Class

This class incorporated some new features compared with the *New Mexico's*. Turbo-electric drive was selected for both ships, the protection below the water line was improved, and the number of medium-caliber guns was reduced. No recesses were built into their hulls for secondary armament casemates. Noticeable aspects of their appearance were a hull line clear of gunports and two funnels. As in previous classes the main battery consisted of 14 in guns mounted in four triple-turrets. Both ships suffered heavy damage at Pearl Harbor and were completely rebuilt. They joined the fleet again totally changed in appearance (see plans). Changes included the addition of hull blisters. The former catapult on turret 'X' was removed.

BB 43 Tennessee

War Service:
1942 Repair to damage sustained at Pearl Harbor. Covering Force Duties off the West Coast and Hawaii. Dockyard repairs.
1943 Covering Force Duties: Aleutians, Kiska, Tarawa.
1944 Kwajalein Majuro, Eniewetok, Kavieng, Saipan, Tinian, Guam, Southern Palau Islands, Leyte, Surigao Straits.
1945 Iwo Jima, Okinawa. Work up period Leyte. Occupation of Japan.

Radar Equipment

	Forward	Aft
1942	Before re-build	
	SC, SRa	
1943	SK	SC-2
1945	SK	SC-2

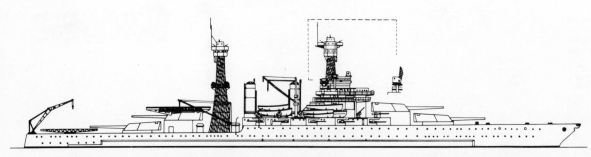

USS *Tennessee* in 1941. There are very few changes to be seen as compared to her original appearance (for a comparison see the section plan of her funnel). Note that her hull line has been cleared of gunports. There are platform-mounted A.A. machine guns atop her masts.

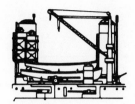

Her funnel section plan up to 1922.

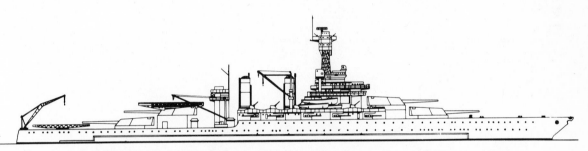

USS *Tennessee* in 1942 in the interval between modifications. Her aft cage mast was replaced by a tower structure. She carried a SRa radar screen in a foretop position. Her A.A. guns were protected by provisional splinter-proof shields.

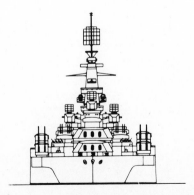

USS *Tennessee* in 1945. A bow view after her total reconstruction. She is now equipped with a SK radar, a fire control radar, and numerous A.A. guns. The 40 mm A.A. four-barrelled gun mount emplaced on top of B-turret is not shown in this drawing. Note her characteristic hull bulges.

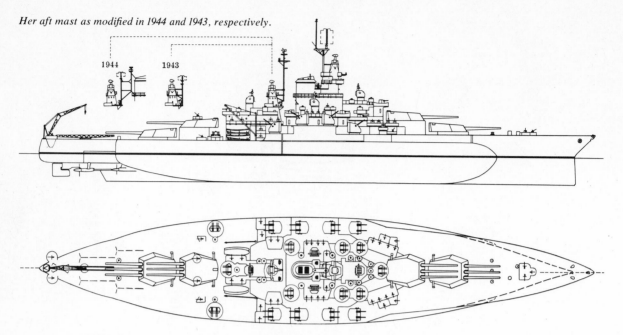

Her aft mast as modified in 1944 and 1943, respectively.

1944   1943

USS *Tennessee* in 1945 after her total reconstruction. There is a certain similarity in appearance to the later *South Dakota II* class, but she has lost all similarity to her own original silhouette.

BB 43 Tennessee

In 1923/24 two of her 5 in L/51 and her submerged torpedo tubes were removed. The number of A.A. guns was increased. In 1929/30 catapults were installed on turret X and on the quarter deck together with aircraft handling gear.

Tennessee was still carrying her two cagemasts at the outbreak of war. She was hit by two bombs at Pearl Harbor, but damage was not serious. In the course of repairs and intermediate modernisation, *Tennessee* received a tall tower structure to replace the old aft cagemast and also splinterproof protection for her A.A. guns.

In October 1942 *Tennessee* went into the dockyard for a major refit, which changed the silhouette of the ship completely. All the superstructure was stripped off, leaving the basic hull and main armament. In its place *Tennessee* received a new and more compact superstructure with a single funnel faired into a tower. The catapult on turret X was not replaced. The hull was fitted with blisters giving the ship an increased beam. Sixteen radar-controlled 5 in L/38 guns were fitted in eight twin-mounts with four Mk 37 fire control equipments. The light A.A. battery received forty 40 mm guns in quadruple mounts.

In August 1944 *Tennessee* was hit three times by coastal artillery off Saipan, and was again damaged in April 1945 by a Kamikaze aircraft.

USS *Tennessee* with three aircraft placed on catapults in the 1930s. Note the saluting guns on top of three of the heavy gun turrets.

Broadside view of USS *Tennessee*. Note her smooth hull as compared to the battleships of former classes and the large base of the aft cage mast.   Collection A. Fraccaroli

USS *Tennessee* in 1942 after the repair of damage suffered at Pearl Harbor. Her aft cage mast has been replaced by a tower structure. The SRa radar antenna is installed atop her foremast. The 5 in A.A. guns are placed behind provisional protective shields. Note the barrage balloons above the ship.

USS *Tennessee* in 1942 after preliminary repair works.

USS *Tennessee* after her total reconstruction. This photograph was taken in May 1943 immediately after her recommissioning. The main radar antennas may either have been erased from the photo by a wartime censor or may not have been installed yet. Four Mk 37 control gear with fire control radars atop are carried. Note the hull bulges forward. The painting is ocean-gray according to Scheme 14.

Broadside view of USS *Tennessee* after her total reconstruction. Note that her appearance has completely changed. Her superstructure resembles the ships of the new *South Dakota (II)* class. Her lower speed excepted, the *Tennessee* could be classified as a modern battleship. Note the SK radar antenna on her foremast and the four Mk 37 fire control equipments carried for her 5 in battery.

BB 44 California

War Service:
1942 Salvaged from Pearl Harbor and totally reconstructed.
1943 Still in the dockyard.
1944 Completion of rebuild. Saipan, Tinian, Guam. Period in dock. Surigao Straits, Leyte.
1945 Lingayen. Period in dock. Okinawa. Occupation of Japan.

Radar Equipment

	Forward	Aft
1941	CXAM	
1944	SK	SP

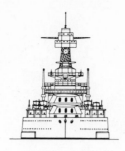

Front view of USS *California* in 1936.

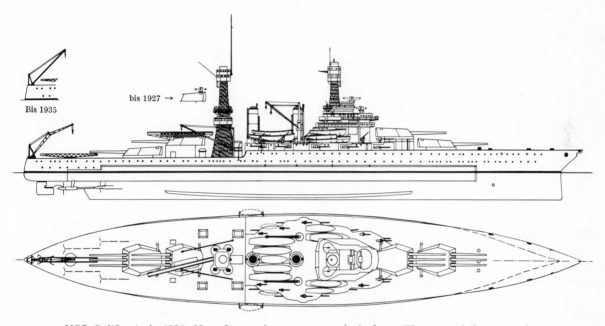

USS *California* in 1936. Her aft mast bears a covered platform. The catapult is mounted diagonally on top of her X-turret.

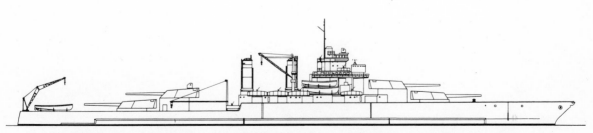

USS *California* in 1942 after repairs and refits following damage at Pearl Harbor. Her bridge now carries a light pole mast. Her cage mast has been completely removed. The A.A. guns are protected by splinter-proof shields.

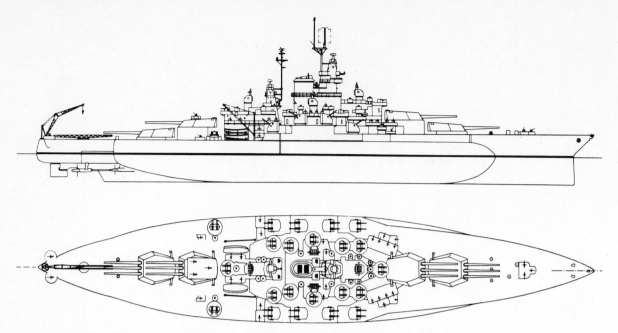

USS *California* in 1945 after her total reconstruction. Only her deck plan reveals changes in the positioning of her 20 mm and 40 mm A.A. guns.

BB 44 California

California's pre-war modifications were similar to those made to *Tennessee*. At Pearl Harbor she was heavily damaged by hits from two torpedoes and three bombs and sank on an even keel. She was raised and provisionally rebuilt. At the same time both the cagemasts were removed and a bridge mounted polemast added. The catapult on turret X was replaced by a rangefinder. All the casemate guns were removed and splinter proof protection was given the A.A. guns.

In 1942 *California* went in for complete modification on the lines of *Tennessee's* and only re-joined the Fleet in May 1944. In June 1944 she was hit by fire from coastal guns and was damaged again by a Kamikaze attack in January 1945.

USS *California* in the 1930s with her crew manning the rails. Note the upper half of her aft cage mast painted black and her very narrow transom.

A model of the *California* exhibited at the San Francisco Maritime Museum showing her midship section.

USS *California* leaving Pearl Harbor after being refloated and repaired following the Japanese attack. Both her cage masts and her catapults are missing. Shortly afterwards the *California* went into dock for total reconstruction.

Photo October 1942. Collection S. Breyer

USS *California* in about 1944 after her reconstruction. Her appearance has completely changed. The three-colour camouflage painting is in accordance with Measure 32. There is no radar antenna recognizable.

Another view of USS *California* after her total reconstruction. She now carries the SK radar antenna on her forward mast head.

Colorado Class

The *Colorado* class was initially nearly identical in appearance to the *Tennessee* class. The principal difference was the adoption of 16 in guns as main armament, arranged in four twin-turrets. Significantly, this caliber of gun had already been introduced on the new Japanese battleships.

Four ships of the *Colorado* class were laid down, but only three completed. Construction of the fourth—*Washington*—was stopped under the terms of the Washington Treaty, and the unfinished hull used as a target for underwater demolition tests.

At the outbreak of hostilities with Japan *Colorado* was in for overhaul at a West Coast yard. *West Virginia* and *Maryland* suffered serious damage at Pearl Harbor. *West Virginia* had to be completely rebuilt,

totally changing her silhouette. She was given a new superstructure exactly resembling the modernized ships of the *Tennessee* class. However, *Maryland*, which had been less damaged, could still be identified as a *Colorado* class battleship after leaving the repair yard.

During World War II only small-sized identification numbers were carried on battleships. It was therefore almost impossible to distinguish between the three similarly converted ships *Tennessee*, *California* and *West Virginia*, even though they belonged to two classes of battleships. However *West Virginia* did retain twin turrets for her main armament, whereas the *Tennessee* class had three-gun turrets. Overall these three ships were considered, after the conversion, as being equivalent to newer battleships, although their speed was less.

BB 45 Colorado

War Service:
1942 Covering Force duty West Coast and South Pacific.
1943 Covering Force duty South Pacific, Tarawa.
1944 Kwajalein, Eniwetok, Saipan, Guam, Tinian, Marcus Islands, Leyte, Mindoro.
1945 Lingayen, Okinawa, Occupation of Japan.

Radar Equipment

	Forward	Aft
1942	SC, SRa	SRa
1945	SK, SRa	

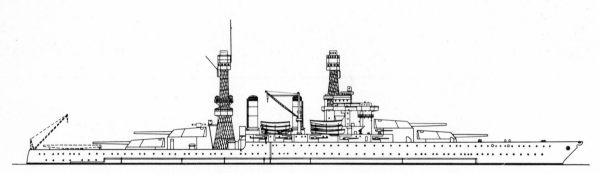

USS *Colorado* in 1923. She was similar in appearance to the *California* and the *Tennessee* except for the 16 in twin-turrets, which the others did not have.

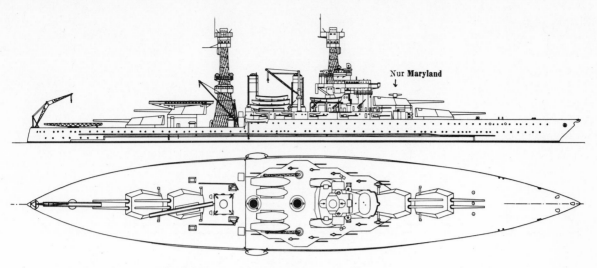

USS *Colorado* in 1937. There have been few changes in the positioning of her A.A. guns. She never carried a range-finder on top of her B-turret.

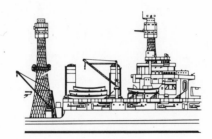

USS *Colorado* at the end of 1941. Her A.A. guns have been concealed behind splinter-proof shields. A.A. machine guns are emplaced on her bridge. The covered platform around her aft cage mast is not shown here.

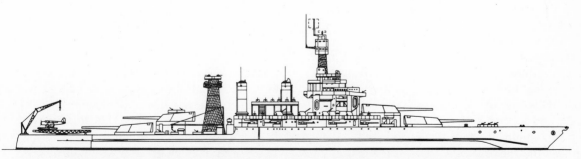

USS *Colorado* in 1943. Her aft cage mast has been shortened and a machine gun platform erected atop the stump. A small funnel cap has been fitted to her forward funnel. Her 5 in L/38 A.A. guns are hidden behind splinter-proof shields. Her forward upper deck 5 in L/51 guns in open mounts have been removed. 20 mm A.A. guns are placed on a "flying platform" around her forward funnel. The ship is equipped with SC and SRa radars rigged in a forward position.

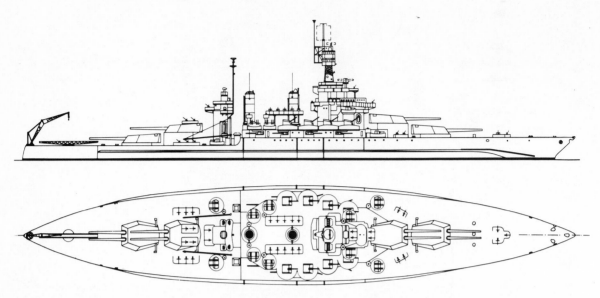

USS *Colorado* in 1945. Her cage mast stump has been replaced by a tower structure aft. Likewise, both her forward 5 in casemate guns have been removed to make room for an increased number of A.A. guns. Her 5 in L/38 guns are now housed in single-mounts. The SK and SRa radars are installed forward, while the SG radar is on her aft mast.

BB 45 Colorado

Colorado's first conversion took place in 1928/29 when the submerged torpedo tubes were removed, and the number of A.A. guns increased. Catapults were fitted on top of turret X and on the quarter deck, and aircraft handling gear was sited by them.

At the outbreak of hostilities *Colorado* was undergoing overhaul at Bremerton, Wash. (West Coast). At that time she was still carrying her two cagemasts. Early in 1942 the aft cagemast was cut down to half its height and a light A.A. gun platform was mounted atop the stump; the fore funnel received a slanted cap, and the 5 in L/25 A.A. guns were replaced by 5 in L/38's with protective shields, (a unique arrangement for this gun hitherto only fitted in open mounts). The remaining deck-sited 5 in L/51 guns were removed to make space for more A.A. guns. In addition two "flying platforms" carrying six 20 mm A.A. guns each were installed on either side of the forward funnel. The X turret catapult was removed and two platforms with two 20 mm A.A. guns each were placed atop the X turret. The light A.A. battery received a total of forty 40 mm and forty-four 20 mm guns.

It was not until 1944 that the aft cagemast stump was removed and replaced by a tower structure. The forward cagemast was retained, but could hardly be recognized as such due to the high bridge structure and the voluminous foretop. The remaining eight 5 in L/51 casemate guns were not removed, but the 5 in L/38's were now mounted in single turrets.

Colorado was damaged three times by enemy action: in July 1944 off Tinian, November 1944 off Leyte by a Kamikaze, and in January 1945 at Lingayen by coastal gunfire.

USS *Colorado* in the 1920s, still without seaplane catapults. Her hull is bare of gunports. Note the hawsehole for her bow anchor.

USS *Colorado* in about 1942, probably painted in a navy-blue colour. Note the SRa radar antenna carried on her foremast platform. The aft cage mast carrying searchlight platforms has not yet been reduced in height.

USS *Colorado* after 1943 with camouflage painting according to Measure 32. Her appearance is similar to the drawing of her in 1943, but now the SK radar antenna has been placed on the foremast.

USS *Colorado* in about 1944 after the replacement of her aft cage mast by a tower structure. The camouflage painting in accordance with Measure 32 prevents the recognition of details, e.g. the "flying platform" on the fore funnel, even at short distances. The hull bulges, however, are clearly visible. Two SRa radar antennas can be recognized. One gun barrel of each of the forward turrets has its muzzle cover on.

USS *Colorado* in 1945 returning from the theatre of war to the US West Coast. Her crew is manning the rails. She still carries her forward cage mast with the SG, SK, and SRa antennas mounted. Her 5 in A.A. guns are still concealed by protective shields.

Photo J. A. Casoly. Collection Fr. Villi

BB 46 Maryland

War Service:

1942 Repair of damage suffered at Pearl Harbor. Covering Force Duty in the East and the South West Pacific.
1943 Covering Force Duty in the South West Pacific. Period in dock. Tarawa. Period in dock.
1944 Kwajalein Majuro. Period in dock. Saipan, Southern Palau Islands, Leyte, Surigao Straits. Period in dock.
1945 In dock. Okinawa. Period in dock.

Radar Equipment

	Forward	Aft
1942	SC	
1944	SK, SRa	SRa

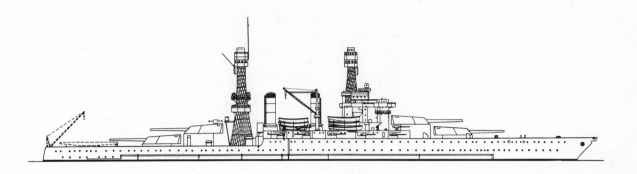

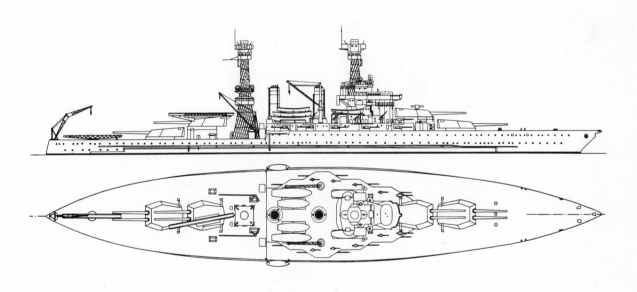

USS *Maryland* at the end of 1941. Her A.A. guns are already protected by splinter-proof shields, but still without radar antenna.

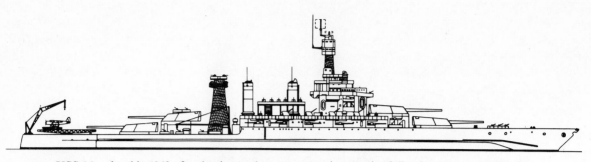

USS *Maryland* in 1943 after having undergone extensive repairs following damage at Pearl Harbor. For details of her aft cage mast stump see the section plan. SC and SRa radars are carried on top of her fore mast.

The aft cage mast stump of the *Maryland* in 1943.

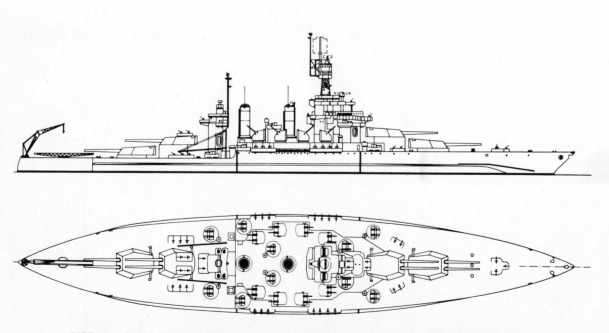

USS *Maryland* in 1945 after her rearmament with eight 5 in L/38 twin-turrets. The platforms for the 20 mm A.A. guns overlap her deck on either side. Her aft cage mast stump has been replaced by a tower structure. She carries SC and SRa antennas on her foretop.

BB 46 Maryland

Pre-war modifications to this ship were similar to those made to *Colorado*. Nor did war time alterations to the two vessels differ greatly, except that *Maryland* was equipped with a total of forty-eight 40 mm A.A. guns, while her final re-armament in 1945 also gave her eight 5 in L/38 A.A. guns set in twin mounts instead of singly. *Maryland* was damaged on three occasions: off Saipan in June 1944 by a torpedo from an aircraft; off Leyte in November 1944; and off Okinawa in April 1945, when a Kamikaze attack caused extensive damage.

USS *Maryland* in the 1930s, recognizable by the range-finder placed atop heavy gun B-turret. She was the first US battleship to be armed with 16 in guns.

Another peacetime photograph of USS *Maryland* in the 1930s. Note the black painting of her aft cage mast above the searchlight platforms. Likewise, note the large number of ship's boats.

USS *Maryland* after the repair of damage suffered at Pearl Harbor. Her aft cage mast has been cut down to half its height and carries a 20 mm A.A. gun platform atop the stump.

Photo November 1942

USS *Maryland* after her second reconstruction during the war. Her aft cage mast has been replaced by a tower structure crowned by a SRa antenna. The SK and another SRa radar antennas are mounted on her foremast. A range-finder and two radar controlled fire control gear are concealed by provisional protective shields. 5 in L/38 single gun mounts have not yet been fitted. The ship is camouflaged in accordance with Measure 12.   Photo April, 1944.

BB 48 West Virginia

War Service:
1942 Sunk at Pearl Harbor; subsequently raised, completely rebuilt.
1942/3 In dockyard under reconstruction.
1944 Training off West Coast. Leyte, Surigao Straits, Mindoro.
1945 Lingayen. Iwo Jima. Okinawa. Occupation of Japan.

Radar Equipment

	Forward	Aft
1941	CXAM	
1944	SK	
1945	SK-2	

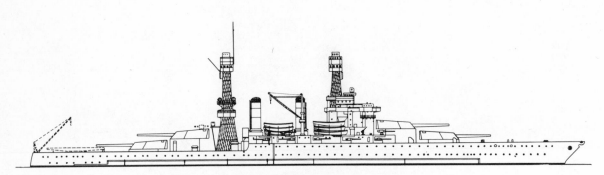

USS *West Virginia* in 1923.

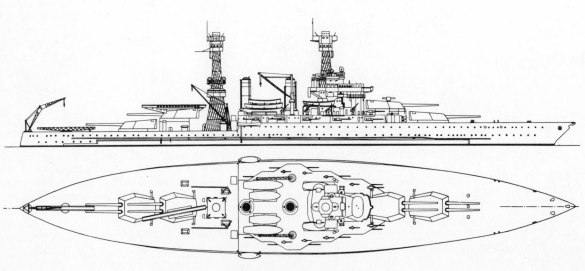

USS *West Virginia* in 1937.

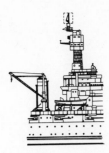

USS *West Virginia* off Pearl Harbor at the end of 1941. A CXAM radar screen is installed on her fore mast. Her A.A. guns have been placed behind splinter-proof shields.

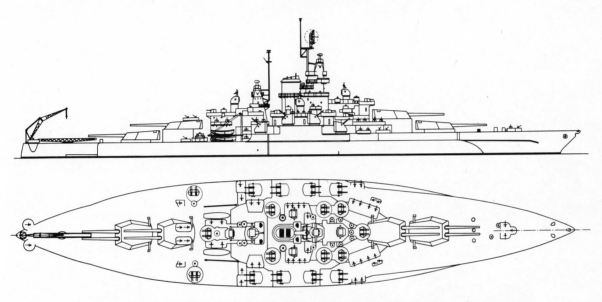

USS *West Virginia* after her total reconstruction. There is very little difference in appearance between this ship and the *Tennessee* although they belong to two different design classes. Besides the calibers of their guns and minor differences in their 20 mm A.A. gun positioning, the *West Virginia* carries four heavy gun twin-turrets whereas the *Tennessee* has four triple-turrets. The SK-2 radar antenna is rigged on the West Virginia's fore mast.

BB 48 West Virginia

The pre-war modifications to *West Virginia* were similar to those made to her sister ships of the *Colorado* class. At Pearl Harbor *West Virginia* was hit by four torpedoes and two heavy bombs. Although severely damaged, she settled on an even keel. After refloating, the ship was totally reconstructed and ceased to resemble her sister ships. The reconstruction followed the lines of the conversion made to the earlier ships *Tennessee* and *California*, to which her appearance became almost identical. However the arrangement of the main armament was different. *West Virginia's* heavy guns were mounted in four twin turrets, whereas *Tennessee* and *California* had four triple turrets. In addition *West Virginia* was fitted with sixteen 5 in L/38 guns, mounted in eight pairs, forty 40 mm A.A. guns and sixty-four 20 mm A.A. guns. She only rejoined the fleet in September 1944, no longer recognizable as a *Colorado* class ship.

West Virginia suffered severe damage on two occasions in action off Okinawa, first from a Kamikaze aircraft in April 1945 and secondly in June 1945 from bombs.

West Virginia was one of the few battleships fitted with the new CXAM radar antenna in 1941, before the Pearl Harbor attack.

Pre-war appearance of USS *West Virginia*. Note the open-mounted 5 in L/51 gun and the minesweeping gear abreast her B-turret, also the awning stanchions and stretchers, and the bow anchor.

Photo August, 1935

USS *West Virginia* after her total reconstruction. She was the only ship of this class reconstructed to the design of the earlier *Tennessee* class. Her camouflage painting is in accordance with Measure 32. She is equipped with a SK antenna.

South Dakota Class I

This book would not be complete without reference to the *South Dakota I* and *Lexington* classes of warships, which were laid down in 1920/21, but the construction of which was suspended as a result of the Washington Treaty of 1922. Totalling twelve ships, these two classes were to incorporate a number of new features of considerable interest. Had the ships been completed they would have considerably altered the balance of the US Fleet at the outbreak of World War II.

South Dakota I was a battleship class, authorised in 1916. However the first ship was not laid down until 1920, after extensive analysis of sea battles during World War I, especially the Battle of Jutland. The first project studies were for a vessel of 80,000 tons with a length of 975 feet, and armed with the exraordinary number of fifteen 18 in guns. The intended maximum speed was 35 knots. Such size and fire-

power was only realised twenty years later with the Japanese battleships of the *Yamato* class. The final design of the *South Dakotas* turned out much closer to that of the *Colorado* class, with about 47,000 tons displacement engines developing 60,000 h.p. and a speed of 23 knots. The main armament consisted of twelve 16 in guns mounted in four triple turrets (this was the heaviest caliber of gun in service at the time). Armor plating was to be one and a half times the thickness of that fitted to the British battlecruiser *Hood*. Overall, the *South Dakotas* were to include many improvements upon the *Colorado* class, although the installation of sixteen boilers caused design problems. In the end they were to be arranged on both sides of the ship alongside the turbines, with four funnels in pairs, which all led into a single main funnel. The drive was to be turbo electric.

The design, as finally released, did not meet the U.S. Navy's requirement for ships to be capable of passing through the Panama Canal.

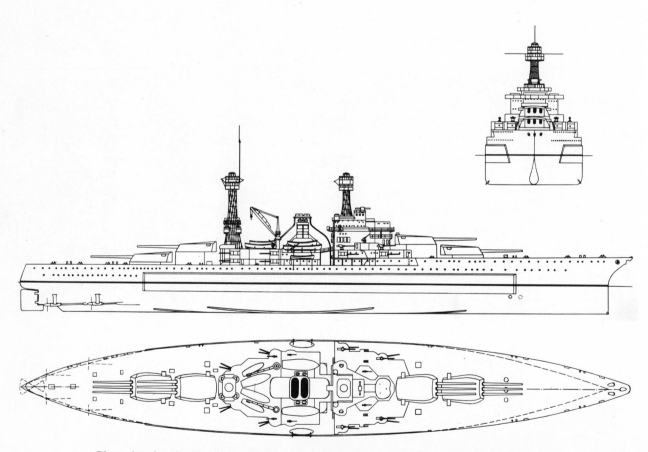

Plans showing the final design of the six *South Dakota I* battleships whose construction was cancelled after World War I. The main battery consisting of 16 in guns is housed in triple-turrets. Note the unique shape of the funnel with quadruple uptakes instead of the four funnels normally needed with the boiler arrangement of these ships. Another new feature was the use of 6 in guns housed in casemate mounts.

"Artist's impression" of the battleships of the *South Dakota (I)* class. Note the 6 in L/53 casemate guns partly mounted on two deck levels.

Lexington Class Battlecruisers (CC)

As had happened before, this design showed the near-impossibility of one type of warship combining superior firepower; adequate protection; and powerful engines to give high speed. The British had originated the conception of the battlecruiser to combine the largest possible number of guns with speed. This concept made armor a secondary feature, because making protection a primary factor in the design inevitably demanded more powerful engines to match the increased weight, which in turn meant the ship's hull had to be larger to accommodate the machinery. Faced with this dilemma, the Americans put their money on protection and striking power, relegating speed to secondary importance.

In contrast the Royal Navy and the Imperial German Navy had developed ships with superior speed—achieved through powerful engines in a high speed hull. The price was having lighter armor and either a smaller caliber of gun, or smaller numbers of guns, than other contemporary battleships possessed. The task of such ships was to destroy inferior warships, whilst keeping out of range of heavy punishment. So it was that the type of ship later called the battlecruiser was born.

As already mentioned, the U.S. Navy showed little interest in this type of warship and the conclusions drawn from the Battle of Jutland delayed decisions on a battlecruiser project. However design work for six ships of the battlecruiser type was started and given consideration in 1916. Two projects were rejected. A third, finalised in 1920, was accepted. The battlecruiser to be built would displace

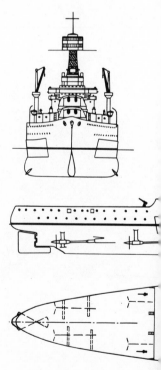

Plans showing the third design of the six *Lexington* class battle-cruisers whose construction was cancelled after World War I. The length of these ships was considerably greater than that of all previous battleships. The medium gun battery of this design was planned to have half its guns in casemates. The torpedo tubes would be installed on the lower quarterdeck. The same applied to the catapults. Two other characteristic features of this design were the bulky funnels and the bow bulge.

49,000 tons, with engines developing 180,000 h.p., giving a projected speed of 33 knots. The main armament was to consist of eight 16 in guns, supported by sixteen 6 in guns. There would be sixteen boilers and turbo-electric drive. The hull line was that of a cruiser and relatively longer than a battleship hull. A large quarterdeck was provided for the subsequent addition of seaplane catapults. An innovation was the bulb bow, introduced after extensive laboratory tests, to reduce water resistance at speeds above 25 knots. Earlier completion of these ships would have made the U.S. Navy the most powerful in the world. But work on them was suspended after the signing of the Washington Treaty, when two—*Lexington* and *Saratoga*—had already been launched. After consultation with the Treaty partners, these hulls were made into aircraft carriers. Conversion work on them started in 1925, *Lexington* being re-classified as

CV 2 and *Saratoga* as CV 3. At 39,000 tons, they became the largest carriers afloat when completed in 1927.

One further attempt was made to add battlecruisers to the U.S. Navy before the end of the 1930's. Six ships of the *Alaska* class were planned, partly in response to the German 'pocket battleships' of the *Deutschland* class and their *Scharnhorst* and *Gneisenau*. The main reason, however, was an unconfirmed report of a Japanese project along similar lines to these German warships. The *Alaskas* had enlarged cruiser hulls, with a battleship superstructure but only nine 12 in guns as main armament. Officially described as 'large cruisers', only two of the six were completed before World War II ended. They were classified as CB I (*Alaska*) and CB 2 (*Guam*)—note the CB classification compared to CC for the *Lexington* class battlecruisers.

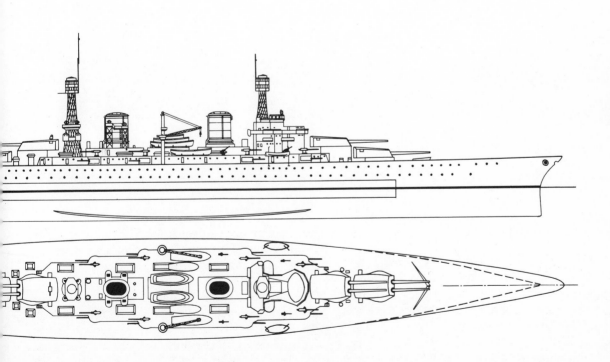

"Artist's impression" of the battle cruisers of the *Lexington* class based on drawings of the third design.

North Carolina Class

The two ships of this class were the first U.S. battleships to be designed, built and commissioned after the end of World War I. They incorporated completely new features and bore little resemblance to their predecessors. For the first time a tower foremast appeared on a U.S. ship. The superstructure was concentrated amidships, which allowed the guns of the main battery a wider arc of fire. The 16 in guns were a new model, while the secondary armament consisted of dual-purpose guns in fully protected twin mounts. The light A.A. guns were set on sponsons with splinter proof shields. (The number of these was increased during the war and they were placed wherever space was available.) Two catapults with associated aircraft handling gear were installed at the stern.

The hull had a rather straighter bow than previous classes and, for the first time in the U.S. Navy, there were no portholes. This was considered advantageous for various reasons (simpler construction, easier damage control, etc.) and carried few disadvantages. The ships' speed of 28 knots was some 2 to 3 knots less than that of contemporary European battleships. Costs were relatively very high, running out at $77 million each (incidentally not enough to pay for a frigate today).

BB 55 North Carolina

War Service:

1942 Training on both East and West Coasts. Guadalcanal. Tulagi. East Solomon Islands. Repairs. Solomon Islands.

1943 Solomon Islands. Covering Force Duties South West Pacific. Gilbert Islands. Kavieng.

1944 Kavieng, Kwajalein Majuro, Truk, Marianas, Palau Islands, Yap Island, Ulithi Island, Woleai, Hollandia, Truk, Satawan, Ponape, Saipan, Philippines. Period in dock. Leyte.

1945 Luzon, Formosa, Chinese coast, Nansei Shoto, Iwo Jima, Honshu, Nansei Shoto, Okinawa. Occupation of Japan.

Radar Equipment

	Forward	Aft
1942	CXAM	
1943	SK	
1945	SK-2	SC-2
1962	SK-2	SP

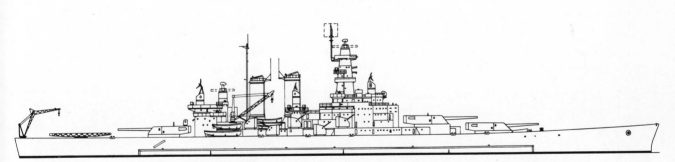

USS *North Carolina* in 1942. Her hull has no portholes. New 16 in gun turrets have been mounted. She was the first battleship to have tower structures instead of masts, and 5 in gun twin-mounts. The 5 in guns mounted were dual purpose guns (DP). The numerous light A.A. guns of later war years had not yet been fitted in 1942. The CXAM radar is installed in a forward position.

BB 55 North Carolina

North Carolina was one of two new battleships which joined the Fleet in 1941. Unlike earlier classes of vessels, which were modernised or converted several times either between the World Wars or after Pearl Harbor, battleships of the *North Carolina* class were not much changed during their active service. What they were given consisted mainly of additional light A.A. guns and improved radar equipment. Thus between April 1941 and June 1942 *North Carolina* had sixteen 28 mm A.A. guns and from twelve to twenty-eight 0.5 in A.A. machine guns. These were then replaced by standard 20 mm and 40 mm A.A. guns with splinter proof protection for the crews, mounted wherever space was available. This re-armament resulted in the installation of certain new mountings for radar, platforms for guns, changes to masts and so on. These improvements meant that minor differences were observable between ships of the same class. Otherwise the only way of distinguishing them was by their different camouflage schemes.

After only six years of active service, in which as her record shows she was hard worked, *North Carolina* was paid off. In 1960 she was struck off the reserve list and became one of the four battleships preserved as memorials. She is now moored at Wilmington, North Carolina.

During her war service *North Carolina* was only once damaged in action. This was when she was hit by a torpedo from a Japanese submarine in September 1942.

USS *North Carolina* as she appeared in June 1942 a few months after her completion, already camouflaged according to Measure 12. In the course of her six years service the *North Carolina* changed her camouflage paint several times: Measure 2—1941, Measure 12—1942, Measure 21—1943, Measure 32—1944, Measure 22—1945/46 and Measure 13—1947. This aerial view clearly shows the arrangement of her 5 in twin-mounts, the different shape of the newly introduced 16 in turrets, and the great number of 20 mm A.A. guns. The 40 mm A.A. guns have not yet been fitted.

USS *North Carolina* showing her small-sized pennant number aft. Two Mk 38 range-finders and four Mk 37 radar controlled equipments are carried. An OS2U "Kingfisher" seaplane is mounted on each catapult.   Photo June, 1942.

USS *North Carolina* at the end of 1944 camouflaged according to Measure 32. Her search and fire control radar equipment has been erased from the photo by a wartime censor.

USS *North Carolina* in August 1946 still wearing her camouflage paint according to Measure 22. Note the SK-2 radar antenna installed on her tower mast. Her funnel caps are painted black.   Collection A. Fraccaroli

USS *North Carolina* as a memorial ship painted "haze gray" according to Measure 13. Note the large-sized pennant number, the SK-2 radar antenna, and the numerous light A.A. guns. The ship rides high in her berth in a port basin near Wilmington, N.C.

BB 56 Washington

War Service:
1942 East Coast. Scapa Flow. Convoy escort to the Soviet Union. Period in dock. Transfer to the Pacific. Guadalcanal.
1943 Guadalcanal. South Solomon Islands. Period in dock. Covering force duty in South West Pacific. Gilbert Islands.
1944 Kavieng. Kwajalein Majuro. Repairs. Marianas Islands. Philippines. Southern Palau Islands. Leyte.
1945 Formosa. Luzon. China Coast. Nansei Shoto. Iwo Jima. Honshu. Nansei Shoto. Okinawa. Period in dock.

Radar Equipment

	Forward	Aft
1942	SC	
1944	SK	
1945	SK-2	SP

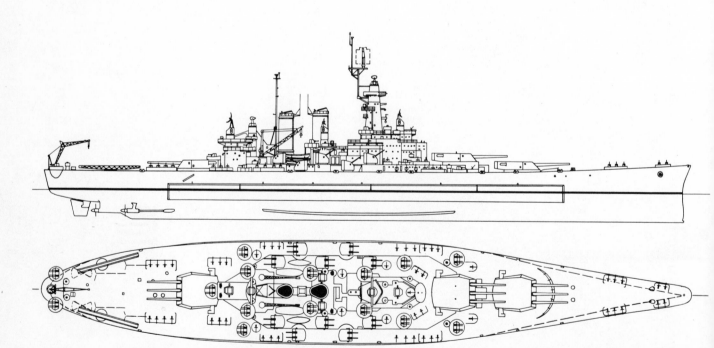

USS *Washington* in 1944 showing numerous light A.A. guns and a SK radar screen on her forward mast. The fire control radar is placed on the Mk 37 gear. Platform-mounted 40 mm A.A. guns are to be seen on top of the aftermost 16 in gun turret. She has two tall funnels placed closely together.

BB 56 Washington

Apart from a collision with *BB 58 Indiana*, which cost her three months of dockyard repairs, *Washington* suffered no damage during the war. As happened with *North Carolina*, the rangefinder in top of the aft 16 in triple gun turret was removed and replaced with a 40 mm A.A. gun platform. This was done in 1942. It had been intended to install an aircraft hangar on the fantail. However this was abandoned on account of the potential fire hazard.

USS *Washington* after her completion, but without the Mk 38 rangefinders. The Mk 4 fire control radar antennas on the four Mk 37 fire control equipments are missing (or were erased by a wartime censor).

USS *Washington* low in the water. Her camouflage paint corresponds to Measure 22. Two Kingfisher reconnaissance seaplanes are carried on the catapults. Note the SK and the two SG radar screens installed.   Photo May, 1944

South Dakota Class (II)

Although the *South Dakotas* had the same beam as the *North Carolinas*, they were shorter vessels. It required more engine power to propel this stubbier hull at the 28 knots which the Navy wanted. At the same time the shorter length provided less hull space. This was compensated for in the design by increasing the width of the first superstructure deck, so that it extended almost the full width of the hull. In consequence additional walkways had to be installed on both sides to facilitate the handling of oil fuelling gear. In turn this led to all the 5 in A.A. gun mounts being placed a deck higher than they were on the *North Carolina* class, and the main superstructure deck being reduced to approximately one third of the length of the hull. This arrangement also increased the firing arc of the main battery. The details can be clearly seen in the drawing opposite.

The time it took to build the four ships of this class was considerably less than had been needed for their predecessors, thanks to improved planning and construction co-ordination.

As can be seen from their War Service records, these ships were utilised in many engagements.

BB 57 South Dakota

War Service:

1942 Commissioned. Sea trials. Santa Cruz. Guadalcanal. Repairs.
1943 Repairs. North Atlantic. Gilbert Islands.
1944 Kwajalein Majuro. Truk. Marianas Islands. Palau Islands. Yap. Ulithi, Woleai. Truk. Satawan. Ponape. Hollandia. Saipan. Philippines. Okinawa. Luzon. Formosa. Ormoc Bay. Mindanao.
1945 China Coast. Nansei Shoto. Iwo Jima. Honshu. Nansei Shoto. Attached to the 5th and 3rd Fleets. Occupation of Japan.

Radar Equipment

	Forward	Aft
1943	2 SRa, SC-2	
1944	SK	

The position of her masts as of 1944, the forward mast carrying a SK radar antenna.

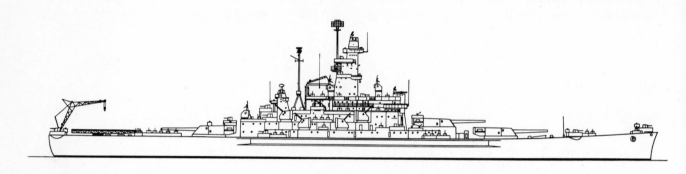

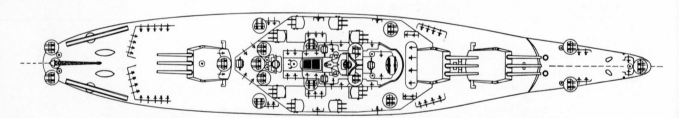

USS *South Dakota* in 1943. Her compact superstructure is concentrated on less than one third of the ship's length. Her funnel is faired into her tower. The SC-2 and the SG radar screens are installed forward and aft respectively. By comparison with her sister ships the *South Dakota* carries two fewer 5 in twin-mounts in the midships position which is partly compensated for by additional 40 mm and 20 mm A.A. guns. On her quarterdeck eighteen 20 mm A.A. guns are emplaced in a so called "hedgehog defense position" between the aftermost heavy gun turret and the catapult. More 40 mm and 20 mm A.A. guns are positioned on top of her aft 16 in gun turret. The arrangement of the three 40 mm A.A. gun stations on her forecastle deck is characteristic of this ship alone.

BB 57 South Dakota

Originally the light A.A. armament of *South Dakota* and her sister ships was to have consisted of 28 mm A.A. guns and 0.5 in machine guns. However this proposal was dropped in favour of 40 mm Bofors A.A. guns. She was given eight more of these than her sister ships, because she was only fitted with sixteen 5 in A.A. guns instead of twenty. These sixteen were in eight twin mountings. Another feature of *South Dakota*, though not a visible one, was that she had additional accommodation to enable her to act as a task force flagship, with the extra personnel that entailed.

In 1943 she operated temporarily with the British Home Fleet. *South Dakota* was the only U.S. battleship to be damaged in a straight fight with an enemy battleship—the Japanese battleship *Kirishima*. During this action in November 1942 she sustained considerable damage. She was also hit by a bomb in June 1944, though with less serious effects. During the battle of Santa Cruz she shot down a total of 26 enemy aircraft.

USS *South Dakota* escorted by a destroyer. The 40 mm A.A. guns in quadruple mounts have replaced the missing 5 in L/38 A.A. guns in twin-mounts on either side. Note the SRa antennas atop her citadel and the Mk 38 range-finder as well as the SC-2 radar screen on her foremast and the SG aft mast. The quadruple mounted 40 mm A.A. guns are covered. Note the arrangement of the three forward 40 mm A.A. gun stations which is characteristic of this ship only. She is painted in accordance with Measure 21. Photo August 1943

USS *South Dakota* in about 1944 painted in "navy-blue". Her SRa antennas had been removed and a SK antenna was installed on her foremast instead.   Collection Fr. Villi

BB 58 Indiana

War Service:

1942 Commissioned. Sea trials. South Pacific.

1943 South Pacific. Marcus and Gilbert Islands.

1944 Kwajalein Majuro. Repairs. Truk. Satawan. Ponape. Marianas Islands. Philippines. Palau Islands. Yap. Ulithi. Philippines. Southern Palau Islands. Period in dock.

1945 In dock. Iwo Jima. Honshu. Nansei Shoto. Attached to the 5th and 3rd Fleets.

Radar Equipment

	Forward	Aft
1943	SC	
1944	SC, SRa	
1945	SK	?

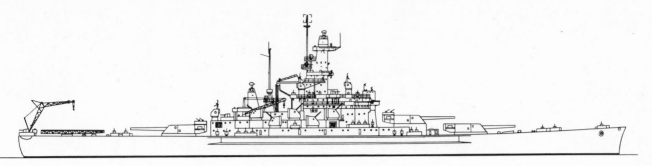

USS *Indiana* in 1942. There are five 5 in twin-mounts on each side. The positioning of her light A.A. guns differs from that of the *South Dakota*. She carries a SC radar antenna on her forward mast.

BB 58 Indiana

Indiana collided with *BB 56 Washington* in February 1944, but did not suffer major damage and was only out of service for a short time. She was never damaged in action.

USS *Indiana* in about 1943. She carries a SC radar antenna on her foremast. Her camouflage painting is in accordance with Measure 22. A light cruiser of the *Cleveland* class can be seen in the background.

USS *Indiana* heading for the Marshall Islands. Note her very compact superstructure, the SRa antenna atop her citadel, and the 40 mm A.A. gun station atop B-turret.

Photo January 1944

USS *Indiana* in three-colour camouflage according to Measure 32. Note the 20 mm A.A. guns atop her aft 16 in gun turret. Both her starboard catapult and the fantail-deck carry an aircraft.

USS *Indiana* in about 1945 camouflaged according to Measure 22. Note the concentration of superstructure in hardly one third of the ship's length and the recess in her side armour amidships.

BB 59 Massachusetts

Radar Equipment

War Service:

1942 Commissioned. Sea trials. North Africa. Period in dock.
1943 In dock. South West Pacific. Gilbert Islands.
1944 Kwajalein Majuro. Truk. Marianas Islands. Palau Islands. Yap. Ulithi. Woleai. Hollandia. Truk. Satawan. Ponape. Period in dock. Southern Palau Islands. Okinawa. Luzon. Cape Engano. Visayas. Formosa.
1945 Formosa. Luzon. China Coast. Nansei Shoto. Iwo Jima. Honshu. Nansei Shoto. Attached to the 5th and 3rd Fleets.

	Forward	Aft
1943	SC-2	
1944	SK	
1965	SK-2	SC-2

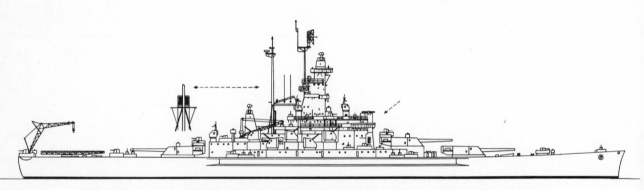

USS *Massachusetts* in 1945 carrying a SK radar screen on her foremast. Due to lack of space she has only a few ship's boats stowed aboard. Note the recess above the vertical armour belt of her hull. There are 40 mm A.A. gun platforms on top of her heavy gun turrets B and Y. As compared to her sister ships she shows minor differences in the design of her tower platform.

Her former open bridge has now been closed in (1945).

BB 59 Massachusetts

In November 1942 *Massachusetts* operated with the joint Anglo-American force supporting the Allied landings in North Africa. During an engagement with the French battleship *Jean Bart*, which was in harbor, she was hit, suffering little damage.

Paid off in 1962, she was later donated to the State of Massachusetts in 1965 and was taken to her final mooring as a memorial ship at Fall River in 1967.

USS *Massachusetts* showing her small-sized pennant number and camouflage paint according to Measure 22. Her SG radar antenna is rigged on her aft mast. Note the fire control radar in a high-angle position on the Mk 37 control gear both forward and aft. Photo July, 1944.

USS *Massachusetts*, around 1946, camouflaged in accordance with Measure 22. The SK-2 radar antenna is installed on her foremast, the SC-2 antenna on her aft mast. The raised 40 mm A.A. gun station on her forecastle deck and the station atop B-turret have already been removed. Note her modified bridge.   Photo J. A. Casoly. Collection Fr. Villi

USS *Massachusetts* resting at her last berth near Fall River, Mass. Note her "haze-gray" peacetime painting, large-sized pennant number, and SK-2 radar antenna on her tower mast.
Photo 1965. Collection S. Breyer

BB 60 Alabama

War Service:
1942 Commissioned. Sea trials.
1943 Sea trials. Covering force duties North Atlantic. South West Pacific. Gilbert Islands.
1944 Kwajalein Majuro. Truk. Marianas Islands.
Palau Islands. Yap. Ulithi. Woleai. Hollandia.
Saipan. Philippines. Guam. Palau. Yap. Ulithi.
Bonin Islands. Southern Palau Islands. Philippines. Okinawa. Luzon. Formosa. Visayas.
Leyte. Luzon.
1945 Period in dock. Attached to the 5th and 3rd
Fleets. Occupation of Japan.

Radar Equipment

	Forward	Aft
1942	SC	
1943	SK	
1945	SK-2	SR
1964	SK-2	SR

Front view of USS *Alabama* showing her hull recess clearly.

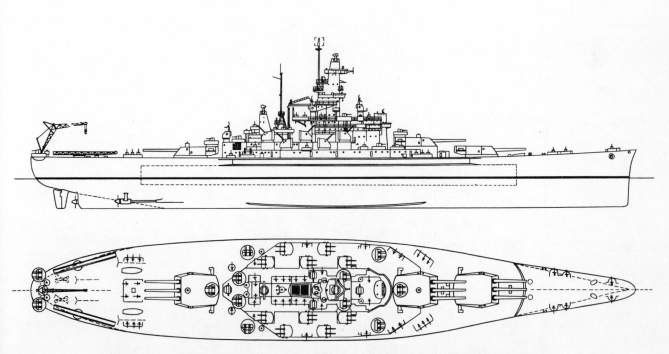

USS *Alabama* in 1943. Note the relatively narrow catwalk on both sides of her main deck.
The light A.A. gun arrangement differs from the disposition on board her sister ships.

BB 60 Alabama

Electronic equipment carried by *Alabama* during her service included two Mk 38 rangefinders for the heavy guns, mounted respectively on the foretop and on top of the aft tower structure—these were supplemented by Mk 8 fire control radars in 1942, which were later replaced by Mk 13 radars. The 5 in A.A. guns were controlled by MK 37 gear, first introduced to battleships in 1941 on *BB 55 North Carolina* and still in use today. The radar associated with this was the Mk 4, later replaced by Mk 22/12.

During 1943 *Alabama* operated with the British Home Fleet in the North Atlantic. After being paid off, the ship was donated to the State of Alabama in June 1964 and moored at Mobile.

Broadside view of USS *Alabama* off the Norfolk Navy Yard. Both the forward 16 in gun turrets are swung to the port side. Note her compact superstructure with the funnel faired into the tower.   Photo November, 1942

USS *Alabama* four months after her commissioning, with camouflage painting according to Measure 12. Some of the 40 mm quadruple A.A. gun mounts to be installed are still missing.
Photo December, 1942

USS *Alabama*: an aerial photo taken at the same time as above. The SC radar antenna is carried on her foremast.
Collection S. Breyer

USS *Alabama* shortly after the end of the war. Note the ship's name painted in large-sized letters on her hull, an identification method used for a short time only. Also note her camouflage painting in accordance with Measure 22, the SK-2 radar antenna on her foremast, and the SRa radar on her aft mast. Mk 13 fire control radar is installed both on the forward Mk 38 rangefinder and on the Mk 38 aft.

USS *Alabama* resting in her present berth near Mobile, Ala., where she is used as a memorial ship. Note the large-sized pennant number and the SK-2 radar antenna.

Photo 1969. Collection Fr. Villi

Midship section of the *Alabama* as a memorial ship. The SK-2 radar antenna has been temporarily removed. Note the comparatively narrow space between her forward and aft masts.   Photo May 1973. H. Pemsel

Close-up view of the *Alabama's* midships section showing the recess above her hull armour. Note the narrow catwalk along her superstructure.   Photo May, 1973. H. Pemsel

Iowa Class

This class demonstrated a relatively new-found capability in American ship design—namely to exploit innovations and so improve dramatically on previous vessels. Thanks to more powerful engines and a significant change in the shape of the hull, the *Iowas* were the fastest battleships in the world.

Whilst the beam remained the same as on earlier ships, so that passage of the Panama Canal was possible, the *Iowas* hulls were longer and relatively more slender than their predecessors. Other benefits accrued from this shape besides speed. There was deck space for more 40 mm and 20 mm A.A. guns than the *South Dakota* class carried (although there was no increase in the medium and large caliber armament). There was more crew room. The ships were also more extensively armored. Yet the resultant increase in displacement of 10,000 tons did not prevent them being faster. It was a considerable achievement.

On a few occasions all four of the *Iowas* operated together as a high speed battleship division. Although they achieved good results in shore bombardment, their main value lay in escorting carrier groups, a role for which their speed and massive A.A. firepower made them particularly suitable. They carried the punch both to ward off attacking Japanese aircraft and to provide protection against enemy surface ships. The *Iowas* proved their efficiency again during the Korean War, when all four were employed to give fire support to the land forces.

Indeed *New Jersey* was re-activated from reserve fleet status in the later Vietnam War for similar duties. During one action off the Vietnam coast she scored incomparably better results than highly sophisticated strike aircraft, whose accuracy was affected by A.A. gunfire during attacks.

All four ships of this class are still listed in the 'Naval Vessels Register' as units of the mothballed reserve fleet. *Iowa* and *Wisconsin* are laid up at Philadelphia, Penn., and *New Jersey* and *Missouri* at Bremerton, Wash. As Reserve Fleet vessels, they are the only battleships in any of the world's navies. However, except for *New Jersey*, they are now in poor general condition. The three others, 'in mothballs' since 1955/58, have been partly cannibalised for spares and damage suffered before they were paid off has not been repaired. Nonetheless, up to the time of writing Congress had still not decided to scrap them. Indeed both *New Jersey* and *Missouri* are earmarked to become memorial ships in their sponsor States. Two other of these $100 million ships were only partially constructed, *BB 65 Illinois* was 22% complete when work on her was stopped in August 1945 and *BB 66 Kentucky* was 69% complete when she was cancelled. The latter was to become the first missile battleship designated BBG 1, but was scrapped in 1958. Both hulls were used as a source for spares. In 1961 their total of four engines, each developing 100,000 h.p., were incorporated in the four fast Combat Support Ships of the *Sacramento* class of 52,000 tons displacement. So powerful was each unit of machinery that they gave the *Sacramentos* a speed of over 26 knots.

The ship's aft funnel in 1953.

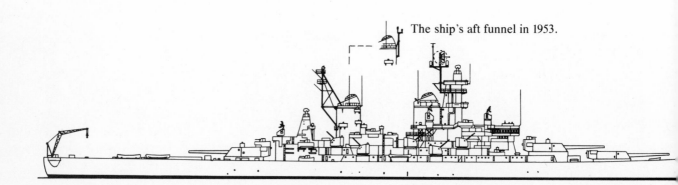

BB 61 Iowa

War Service:

1942 Under construction.

1943 Commissioned. Sea trials. Covering force duty North Atlantic. Sailed with President Roosevelt aboard across the Atlantic to the Teheran Conference. Return to the United States.

1944 Kwajalein Majuro. Truk. Marianas Islands. Mille. Palau Islands. Yap. Ulithi. Woleai. Hollandia. Truk. Satawan. Ponape. Saipan. Philippines. Guam. Tinian Island. Palau Islands. Yap. Ulithi. Philippines. Southern Palau Islands. Okinawa. Luzon. Formosa. Visayas.

1945 In dock. Okinawa. Occupation of Japan.

1951/2 Re-activated for service Korea.

Radar Equipment

	Forward	Aft
1943	SK, SRa	
1945	SK-2,	SC-2
	1950	SPS 6
SP	1952	SPS 6
SP	1958	SPS 6
SPS 8A		

 USS *Iowa* in 1948 carrying a SK-2 radar screen. All 20 mm A.A. guns have been removed. Her aft mast is supported by her aft funnel. Her quarterdeck-mounted catapult has been removed.

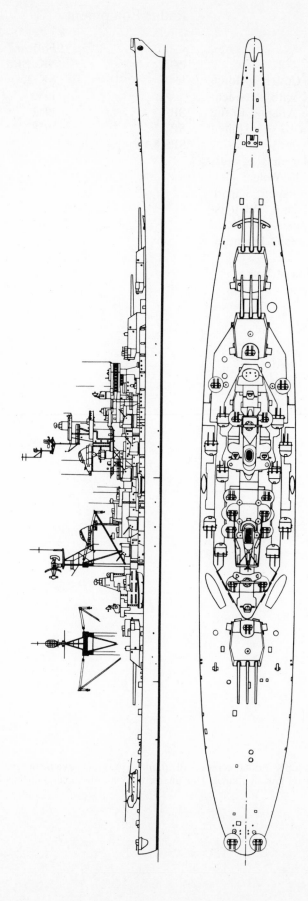

USS *Iowa* in 1958 before being paid off after her second active service period. The SPS 6 radar antenna is carried in a forward position while the SPS 8A screen is rigged on her aft mast. Her quarterdeck has been cleared and her aircraft handling crane removed to make room for helicopter operations. In 1945 she was equipped with a SC-2 radar antenna rigged on a light tripod mast that had been mounted on her aft funnel. The aft masts and the topmasts were modified several times in ships of this class.

BB 61 Iowa

Nine months after her completion, President Roosevelt used *Iowa* to take him across the Atlantic to Casablanca for his participation in the Teheran Conference of November 1943. During the voyage *Iowa* had a near-miss from a torpedo fired accidentally by a U.S. Navy destroyer. Her only actual war damage came in March 1944 when she was with the Pacific Fleet and was hit by two shells from Japanese coastal guns. The damage was slight.

Iowa, together with her sister ships *New Jersey* and *Wisconsin*, remained in service for four years after the end of World War II. After a short period with the reserve fleet, she re-joined the active fleet after the outbreak of hostilities in Korea in 1951. She was paid off for a second time in 1958.

Consideration was given at various times to ways of making use of these relatively new and expensive ships in the post-war Navy. At the end of the 1950s, when Intercontinental Ballistic Missiles (ICBM) were being fitted into submarines (SSBN), there was a plan to turn the battleships into 'high speed missile monitors', with their heavy gun turrets replaced by missile launchers. Indeed the last ship of this class, *BB 66 Kentucky*, had her construction suspended when she was already 69 percent complete and had been floated out of dock. She was to have been made into the first missile battleship, with the designation BBG 1.

In the early 1960s plans were made for the *Iowas* conversion into Amphibious Command Ships. This would have involved removing the aft heavy gun turret and half the machinery to make space for the accommodation of twelve transport helicopters and 1,200 Marines.

All these plans were eventually dropped because of lack of Congressional support for the necessary expenditure. *Iowa* was mothballed without her 40 mm guns, the spaces being left empty.

One of the few "family portraits" of the *Iowa's* showing "Battleship Division Two" during active service after the Korean War. The photo was taken in June 1954 eight months prior to the decommissioning of USS *Missouri*. USS *Iowa* leads USS *Wisconsin*, USS *Missouri*, and USS *New Jersey*.

USS *Iowa* two months after her commissioning anchoring off the New York Naval Shipyard. She already carries an SK radar antenna on her foremast. The 40 mm A.A. guns are covered.

Photo April, 1943

USS *Iowa* with all her A.A. gun barrels elevated. Her camouflage paint follows Measure 22. Her raised fantail deck does not run parallel to the water line and is therefore painted haze-gray instead of navy-blue.   Photo November, 1943

Slightly oblique forward view of the *Iowa* approximately at the beginning of 1944. The camouflage painting has been changed. The ship is making slow speed. The crews manning the forward 20 mm A.A. gun stations are highly exposed to breaking waves.
                           Collection S. Breyer

"Peaceful" photograph of the *Iowa* in October 1952 during the Korean War. All 20 mm A.A. guns and part of the A.A. gun stations as well as the catapults have been removed. She already has black funnel caps and a large-sized pennant number. Note the identification pennant number "61" underlined for correct air recognition on A-turret and the "Stars and Stripes" painted on B-turret. A SPS 6 radar is carried on her forward mast top, SP radar on her aft mast.

An impressive aerial view of the two sister ships, USS *Iowa* (with ammunition stowed on her quarterdeck) and USS *Missouri* (still showing a small-sized pennant number), in a Far East port. Note the fantail-sited boat stowage racks. The *Missouri* carries a newer fire control radar equipment with the Mk 37 gear than the *Iowa* does. The photograph also shows a landing craft utility (LCU). It is interesting to compare the size of this landing craft with the size of the battleships. 				Photo October, 1952

BB 62 New Jersey

War Service:

1942	Under construction.
1943	Commissioned. Sea trials.
1944	Kwajalein Majuro. Truk. Palau Islands. Yap. Ulithi. Woleai. Mille. Hollandia. Truk. Satawan. Ponape. Saipan. Philippines. Palau Islands. Yap. Ulithi. Guam. Southern Palau Islands. Philippines. Okinawa. Luzon. Visayas. Formosa. Luzon.
1945	Formosa. China Coast. Nansei Shoto. Luzon. Honshu. Nansei Shoto. Iwo Jima. Attached to the 5th and 3rd Fleets. Period in dock. Occupation of Japan.
1950/51	Re-activated for service, Korea.
1968/69	Re-activated for service, Vietnam

Radar Equipment

	Forward	Aft
1943	SK	
1945	SK-2	SP
1951	SPS 6	SP
1956	SPS 6	SPS 8A
1968	SPS 6	

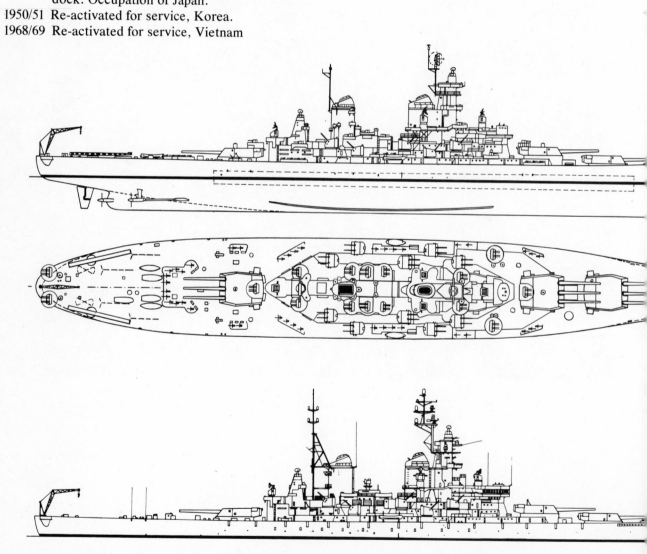

146

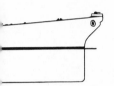

USS *New Jersey* in about 1945 still carrying both her catapults. Her SK-2 radar can be seen in a forward position. She is armed with numerous 20 mm A.A. guns mainly emplaced on her main deck. She still has a pole mast supported by her aft funnel.

USS *New Jersey* in 1968/1969. The plan shows the ship during her third active service period. A heavy communications aerial has been installed on her forecastle deck. All her 40 mm A.A. gun countersunks are empty and the sponsons on top of her turrets B and Y have been removed. Her Mk 37 fire control gear has received updated radar screens. Two additional Mk 56 fire control equipments are placed between her funnels. Her foretop has been modified to accommodate the sophisticated ECCM aerials. Her foremast shows several newly mounted platforms for the ECM aerials. Her aft mast has been reinforced by supports although it only bears some light IFF antennas. The SPS 6 and 10 radar screens are placed forward. The aircraft handling crane has been retained to handle the ship's boats. A number of whip aerials are carried on, and/or attached to, her bridge, funnels and fantail.

Front view of her modified top with the ECCM frames.

BB 62 New Jersey

After the war *New Jersey* was paid off in August 1948 and laid up with the Reserve Fleet until November 1950. Her first re-activation for the Korean War led to six year' active service until 1957, when she was again paid off and laid up at Philadelphia. Ten years after this, in 1967, came her second re-activation, when the Vietnam War called for long range heavy guns capable of highly accurate fire. However she served on only one mission as a fire support ship in Vietnam's coastal waters. In 1969 she was paid off again, mothballed for a second time, and laid up with the Reserve Fleet at Bremerton, Wash. Various minor changes made during her third period of active service are noticeable on photographs taken at the time—see the following pages.

In the early 1950s it was planned to replace *New Jersey's* 40 mm A.A. guns with the newly introduced radar controlled 3 in L/50 twin mounted guns. So far as is known this replacement was not carried out, though it may have been carried out on *Iowa* and *Wisconsin*. But all four ships of this class did have their 40 mm A.A. guns during their first and second active duty periods. When *New Jersey* was paid off for the second time in August 1957 all her 40 mm guns were intact. When she was finally paid off ten years later the light A.A. armament had been removed. Only the empty positions for these guns were left.

Aerial view of the *New Jersey* from astern in the Puget Sound area shortly before the end of the war. The SK-2 antenna is already mounted forward and a SP screen is on the aft mast.
Photo June, 1945. Collection S. Breyer

An interesting and unusual detail view of the *New Jersey*. Her aft funnel cap is painted gray instead of black and there are rails around it. The SG radar antenna can be seen clearly. Platform-mounted searchlights are attached to the funnel. A Kingfisher reconnaissance plane is just being launched from her port catapult.   Photo November, 1943

USS *New Jersey* shortly after her commissioning. The 20 mm A.A. gun stations are not installed yet. A SK radar antenna is mounted on her foremast whereas a SG radar antenna is on her aft mast.   Photo 1943

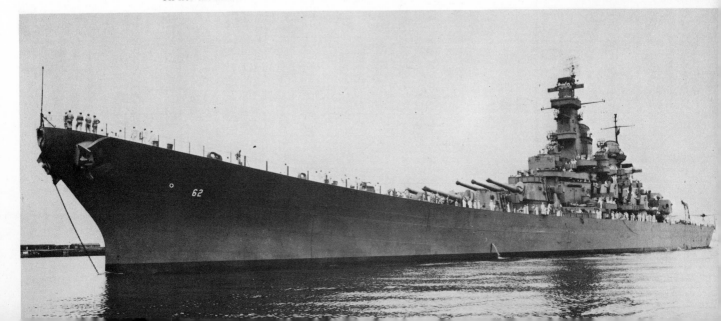

USS *New Jersey* shortly before the end of the war camouflaged according to Measure 22. A SG radar has been mounted above the SK-2 screen.   Collection Fr. Villi

USS *New Jersey* in the post-war years between 1946 and 1948. This is a very interesting and impressive photograph showing the ship in peacetime gray. There have been no changes made to her armament and equipment since 1945. The funnel cap is now painted black. The catapults and aircraft are still carried.   Collection S. Breyer

Mothballing the *New Jersey* after her first decommissioning. The 20 mm A.A. guns and the midship-sited 40 mm A.A. guns have been removed (the stations are partly empty). The remaining 40 mm guns, the 5 in mounts and the 16 in turrets have already been sealed. All the electronics equipment, however, is still on board the ship. The starboard catapult has been removed, its ring mount still being visible. Photo June, 1949

USS *New Jersey*, the first of the three sister ships to be reactivated for service off the Korean coast. The photograph shows the ship without her former 20 mm A.A. guns, but with 40 mm A.A. guns re-installed. She carries the same electronics equipment as in 1945. The small-sized pennant number has not been changed. The ship's boats occupy the place of the former catapult.   Photo July, 1951. Collection S. Breyer

Midship section view of USS *New Jersey* visiting Toulon in Southern France during her second period of active service. Her aft mast reinforced by a supporting structure carries the SPS 8A radar antenna. The SPS 6 antenna is installed on her fore mast. Likewise, a new fire control radar on the Mk 37 gear and additional Mk 56 control gear units have been mounted. The Mk 56s are placed in front of the aft funnel, beside the tower mast, and on the supporting structure of the aft mast.   Photo October, 1955, M. Bar

USS *New Jersey* after her second re-activation in 1968. Note the large-sized pennant number which had already been changed before her previous paying off. A long-distance communications antenna anchored to the deck edges has been installed on the forecastle. The 40 mm A.A. gun positions, some of which were later removed, are not occupied by guns. There is a "highline" transfer gear on top of B-turret. The fantail deck has been cleared for helicopter operations. The 16 in battery and the 5 in guns have been re-activated.

A detailed view of the *New Jersey's* forward funnel/bridge section. The funnel is faired into the tower structure. Note that there are five deck levels, from the maindeck upwards to the signal bridge. All light A.A. gun stations have been cleared of their weapons. Abaft the mast some ECM antennas are installed; the uppermost screen is a SPS 10 radar antennae, followed by a SPS 6. Note the modified fore top below the Mk 38 range-finder. Two bridge deck levels are discernible, one of them being for the Admiral.   Photo 1968. Collection S. Breyer

USS *New Jersey* returning from sea trials prior to her third commissioning. Her fore top has again been modified. ECCM antennas are suspended on either side.   Photo March, 1968

An impressive front view of the *New Jersey*. Note the two huge anchors and the water outlets along the plating. In front of, and to the side of, the tower mast there are three Mk 37 fire control equipments for the 5 in battery, all placed on one deck level.   Photo March, 1968

BB 63 Missouri   Radar Equiment

War Service:
			Forward	Aft
1942	Under construction.	1944	SK-2	
1943	Under construction.	1947	SK-2	SP
1944	Commissioned. Sea trials.	1950	?	SP
1945	Sea trials. Honshu. Nansei Shoto. Iwo Jima.	1950	SG-6	SP
	Okinawa. Occupation of Japan.	1951	SPS 6	SP
1950/52	Korea.	1954	SPS 6	SPS 8A

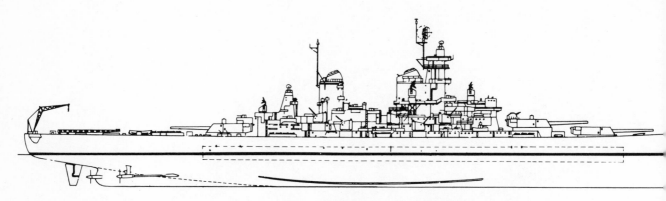

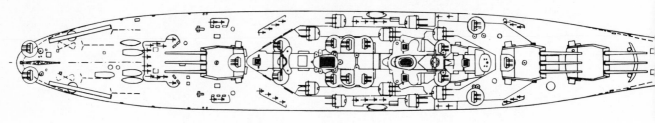

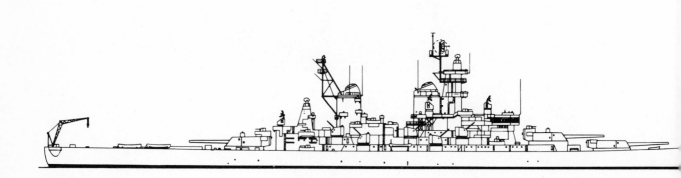

BB 63 Missouri

In April 1945 *Missouri* was slightly damaged by Kamikaze aircraft off Okinawa. She became famous a few months later when the Japanese surrender was signed on board on September 2nd 1945. During the Korean war she was the only ship to be carrying a SG-6 radar antenna, which was mounted on the top of the mast on the forward tower structure.

Missouri was the only ship of the *Iowa* class to see continuous service with the Fleet from World War II on until after the Korean War. When she was laid up in 1955 her 40 mm quadruple gun mounts were left intact.

USS *Missouri* in 1945.

USS *Missouri* as of 1947 after the removal of her 20 mm A.A. guns and her catapult. The SK-2 radar antenna is mounted forward whereas the SP aerial is aft. Her funnel mast has been modified.

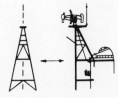

Her aft mast as of 1951 reinforced by additional supports to carry the SPS 8A antenna.

USS *Missouri* riding high at anchor off New York Naval Shipyard one month after her commissioning. She is already camouflaged according to Measure 12. When commissioned she was equipped with the SK-2 radar antenna seen on her foremast. Note the aircraft handling crane in its lowered position. Photo July, 1944

USS *Missouri* one month later. Note the different camouflage painting pattern on her port and starboard sides. The black smoke may be caused by the crew cleaning the boilers. Photo August, 1944

A model of the *Missouri*. This instructive photograph allows a comparison with the *New Jersey's* detailed view showing the latter's forward funnel/bridge section. The *Missouri* carries the SK-2 antenna on her mast. The Mk 38 range-finder is still linked with the older Mk 8 fire control radar whereas the Mk 37 control gear is equipped with a Mk 22/12 fire control radar. There are visual target finders for the 40 mm A.A. guns, the 20 mm and 40 mm A.A. gun stations, and a ladder attached to the funnel.　　　　Photo U.S. Navy

USS *Missouri* with all hands on deck celebrating the fourth anniversary of Japan's surrender, which was signed aboard this ship. Note the wide base of her citadel and the 40 mm A.A. gun station atop B-turret. Four life rafts are attached to either side of the turret. Each of the 16 in gun turrets is equipped with its own range-finder.

USS *Missouri* in the Mediterranean prior to the Korean War. At that time she was the only US battleship on active duty. Note the MK 13 fire control radar added to the range-finders and the Mk 56 fire control gear for the 40 mm A.A. guns. Her aft mast has received SP and SG radar antennas. Her fore mast was then equipped with an antenna still unknown to the public. Only a few prototypes of this antenna were installed, the one of the *Missouri* soon being removed. Note the funnel cap painted black. Photo 1950, M. Bar

USS *Missouri* some months later off Chong Jin, Korea, firing a 16 in gun salvo at enemy inshore installations, only 39 miles from the border of China. Note the 20 mm A.A. bow guns of her World War II armament still in place. She still has her small-sized wartime pennant number. Her foremast temporarily received a SG 6 radar antenna which was never installed on any other battleship. Photo October, 1950

USS *Missouri* mothballed at Bremerton, Wash. Note the large-sized pennant number and the funnel caps painted gray. The dome-shaped coverings of the 40 mm A.A. gun stations show that the guns have been mothballed too. All of her electronics equipment, however, was removed beforehand. The bridge windows are closed by blinds. Of all the battleships of this class the *Missouri* was paid off only once.

BB 64 Wisconsin

War Service:

1942	Under construction
1943	Under construction
1944	Commissioned. Sea trials. Accompanying fast aircraft carriers in the Pacific. Luzon.
1945	Formosa. China Coast. Nansei Shoto. Luzon. Honshu. Nansei Shoto. Iwo Jima. Attached to the 3rd and 5th Fleets. Occupation of Japan.
1951/52	Re-activated for service, Korea.

Radar Equipment

	Forward	Aft
1944	SK	
1947	SK	SC-2
1952	SPS 6	SPS 8A
1954	SPS 6	SPS 8A
1957	SPS 6	SPS 8A

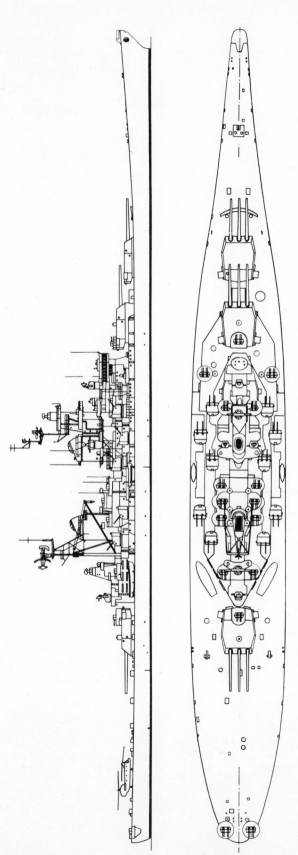

USS *Wisconsin* in 1958. The plan shows the ship shortly before her final paying off. The SPS 6 radar antenna is forward and the SPS 8A radar on her additionally supported aft mast. All her 40 mm A.A. guns are still mounted. Her aircraft handling crane has been removed. The handling hoists for her ship's boats are installed on either side abreast her aft funnel.

Rear view of her aft mast with the hoists for handling the ship's boats.

BB 64 Wisconsin

Wisconsin was mothballed in July 1948 after post-war service with the Fleet. She remained on the reserve until March 1951, when she was re-activated for the Korean War. During this war she alternated with her three sister ships in providing naval gunfire support to the ground forces. At this time she still carried quadruple mounted 40 mm A.A. guns, although other types of ship had by then been re-armed with the 3 in L/50.

In May 1956 *Wisconsin* collided with the destroyer *DD 510 Eaton* and sustained considerable damage to her bow. Repair was effected by replacing the whole bow section with that from the incomplete *BB 66 Kentucky* (which was eventually scrapped in 1958). *Wisconsin* was finally paid off in 1958.

USS *Wisconsin* in her two-colour paint scheme towards the end of the war. The ship's name on the stern transom has been painted over. Note the two 40 mm A.A. mounts on the sponsons on either side of the aircraft handling crane. The SK radar antenna is carried on her foremast, the SC-2 and SG antennas are installed on her aft pole mast.

An impressive detailed photograph of USS *Wisconsin*'s forward section showing her forward 16 in gun barrels with muzzle covers and her tower mast. There is a breakwater in front of her A-turret. The SPS 6 radar antenna has been installed abaft the Mk 38 range-finder on the mast top.

Photo March, 1952

Aerial view of the *Wisconsin* during an overhaul. She was drydocked in an AFDBI (Large Auxiliary Floating Drydock) which still appears too short to take the whole ship. Note the slim forecastle of the *Wisconsin*. Due to the arrangement of her engines the ship's greatest width seems to be too far aft. Her funnel caps are painted black.   Photo April, 1952

USS *Wisconsin* operating with the Atlantic Fleet after the end of the Korean War. Note the large-sized pennant number, the new radar for the Mk 37 fire control gear, the SPS 6 antenna on her foremast, and the SPS 8A antenna on her aft mast. The latter has been strengthened by supports.   Photo January, 1955

Broadside view of USS *Wisconsin* in 1956 fully dressed in honour of George Washington's birthday. She is anchored off the Cuban coast. Note the additional supporting structure for her aft mast, the helicopter on her quarterdeck, and the 40 mm A.A. guns still mounted. The shadows in bright tropical sun reveal the overhang of her forecastle. The aircraft handling crane has already been removed.

USS *Wisconsin* passing the entrance to New York Harbour ten months before being paid off. The ship's name is clearly visible on the stern transom from which the ladder has been removed.   Photo May, 1957. Collection S. Breyer

Philadelphia Naval Shipyard 1967: The *Wisconsin* has left the refitting berth to make room for USS *New Jersey* to be towed in by tugs. USS *Iowa* can be seen in the far left of this photograph. Prior to her mothballing all 40 mm A.A. guns were removed from the *Wisconsin* while the *New Jersey*, as seen here, is still carrying them. There are also two mothballed aircraft carriers in the background, the *Antietam* (CVS 36) and the *Cabot* (AVT 3).

Montana Class

This class of five projected ships reached the final design stage but was never built. The main armament would have been twelve 16 in guns mounted in four triple turrets. The ships' speed was to be 28 knots. These qualities were reckoned at the time to make the *Montanas* at least the equal of the Japanese *Yamato* class. The Americans were ignorant of the details of newer Japanese battleships then under construction, but their strategic concepts included other factors besides matching the speed and armament of individual enemy ships. In particular the U.S. Navy considered that a greater number of battleships would compensate for any comparative deficiency of firepower, whilst a large number of aircraft carriers would provide air superiority for the U.S. Fleet.

In the end American experience with carriers, revealing the overwhelming value of air superiority, led to the cancellation of orders for the *Montana* class in July 1943. Instead six large aircraft carriers (CVB) of the *Midway* class were ordered, three of which were completed and commissioned and the other three cancelled when the war with Japan ended.

Had the *Montanas* been built, they would have been five of the most powerful battleships ever known. One limiting factor on size had always been the requirement for passage through the Panama Canal, which set the ship's maximum beam. For the first time in the U.S. naval history this requirement was waived, so that the *Montanas* could be larger. Their designed displacement was a colossal 65,000 tons, greater than any existing battleship. Their intended speed was 33 knots, equal to that of the *Iowas*, which meant having an even longer hull to achieve the necessary slender hull shape, as well as having even more powerful engines. The final projected hull length of 925 feet was going to cause problems over building dock capacities. Further features of the design were improved underwater protective armor, and the introduction of a new model of 5 in dual purpose gun with a barrel length of fifty-four times its caliber.

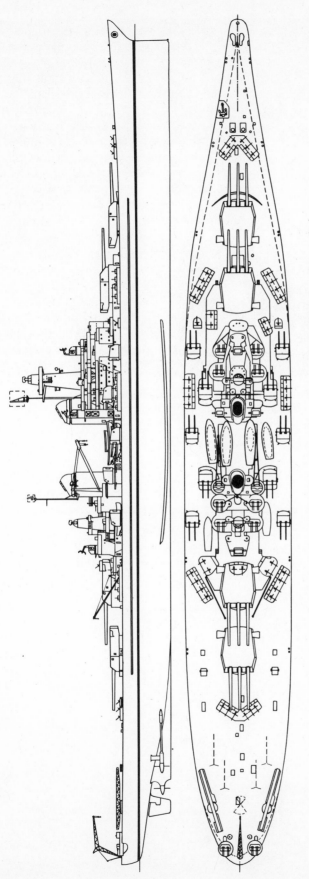

Montana class battleships, the construction of which was cancelled. The plan shows their intended appearance with four 16 in gun triple-turrets according to the final design of 1942/43. The arrangement of the 20 mm A.A. guns and the type of radar equipment shown is probably hypothetical only. The turrets planned to house the new 5 in L/54 A.A. guns show no recognizable differences from former turret designs.

A model of the *Montana* class showing general appearance only. Note the unique and rather strange shape of the radar antenna, the four 16 in gun turrets, and the single catapult to starboard. The midship section resembles that of the *Iowa* class.   Collection S. Breyer

An artist's impression of the *Montana* class battleships showing their likely appearance had they been completed before the end of the war. Particulars shown are possibly based on the final design drawing though some details are taken from the *Iowa* class battleships.

Ship names in standard print refer to the short history of
each ship. Ship names in italics refer to the classes of ships.

Bibliography

BOOKS

Breyer, S.: Schlachtschiffe und Schlachtkreuzer 1905–1970, J. F. Lehmanns Verlag, München, 1970

Coker, P. C.: Building Warship Models, Charleston, 1974

Ellis, C.: Warship Camouflage 1939–1945, Pique Publications, Kirstall Productions Ltd., Henley-on-Thames, 1975

Giorgerini, G.: Le navi da battaglia della seconda guerra mondiale, Ermanno Albertelli Editore, Parma, 1972

Japanese Battleships and Cruisers: Macdonald, London, 1963

Jentschura/Jung/Mickel: Die japanischen Kriegsschiffe, J. F. Lehmanns Verlag, München, 1970

Leifer, N.: Dreadnought returns, Baum Printing House, Inc., Philadelphia, Penn., 1969

Lenton, H. T.: American Battleships, Carriers, and Cruisers, Macdonald & Co. Ltd., London, 1968

Naval History Division (Department of the Navy): The Battleship in the United States Navy, Washington, D.C., 1970

Pemsel, H.: Von Salamis bis Okinawa, J. F. Lehmanns Verlag, München, 1975

Rohwer/Hümmelchen: Chronik des Seekrieges 1939–1945, Gerhard Stalling Verlag, Oldenburg und Hamburg, 1968

Ruge, Fr.: Entscheidung im Pazifik, Dulk-Verlag, Hamburg, 1951

Silverstone, P. H.: U.S.-Warships of World War II, Ian Allan, London, 1965

U.S. Government Printing Office: United States Naval Aviation 1910–1970, Washington, D.C., 1970

Watts, A. J.: Japanese Warships of World War II, Ian Allan, London, 1966

Wetterhahn, A.: Flotten-Revue 1948 Band I und II: USA, seinerzeitiger Vertrieb Paul Schmalenbach Bremen, 1948/49

REFERENCE YEARBOOKS

Blackman/McMurtrie: Jane's Fighting Ships, annual publication, Macdonald, London

Bredt/Weyer: Taschenbuch der Kriegsflotten, verschiedene Jahrgänge, J. F. Lehmanns Verlag, München

Fahey, J.: Ships and Aircraft of the U.S. Fleet, annual publication, U.S. Naval Institute (Falls Church and Annapolis).

Leeward Publications: vol. 1: USS North Carolina, 1973; vol. 2: USS Alabama, 1974, Pearl Harbor Attack, 1974

Naval History Division (Department of the Navy): Dictionary of American Naval Fighting Ships, Vols. I–V, 1950–1970, Washington, D.C.

Warship Profiles: Vol 21 USS Tennessee

PERIODICALS

Davis, W. H.: Ship list, U.S.-Navy, reproduced in The Belgian Shiplover, Brussels

Fisher, E. C.: Warship International, Toledo, Ohio

Ishiwata, K.: Ships of the World, Kaijinsha & Co., Tokyo

U.S. Naval Institute Proceedings: Annapolis, Md.

Tabulated Ship Data

Construction data, armor, and propulsion

Penn. No.	Name of the ship	F.Y.	Laid down	Launched	Commissioned	Decommissioned	Paid off	Build. Yard	Fate
32	Wyoming	09	9. 2.10	25. 5.11	25. 9.12	as BB: 1.1.31 as AG: 1.8.47	16. 9.47	Cramp. Philad.	Scrapped
33	Arkansas	09	25. 1.10	14. 1.11	17. 9.12		25. 7.46	N.Y.S.B. Camden	Sunk as target for nuclear tests
34	New York	10	11. 9.11	30.10.12	15. 4.14	29. 8.46	8. 7.48	N.Y.N. Shipyard	Sunk as target for nuclear tests
35	Texas	10	17. 4.11	18. 5.12	12. 3.14	21. 4.48		Newport News S.B.&D.D.	Now relic at Houston, Texas
36	Nevada	11	4.11.12	11. 7.14	11. 3.16	29. 8.46	31. 7.48	Fore River, Quincy	Sunk as target for nuclear tests
37	Oklahoma	11	26.10.12	23. 3.14	2. 5.16	7.12.41	17. 5.47	N.Y.S.B. Camden	Hulk sunk during towing operation
38	Pennsylvania	12	27.10.13	16. 3.15	12. 6.16	29. 8.46	10. 2.48	Newport News S.B.&D.D.	Sunk as target for nuclear tests
39	Arizona	13	16. 3.14	19. 6.15	17.10.16		7.12.41	New York Nav.Sh.	Sunk at Pearl Harbor; now relic

BB	Class	Armor in mm								
		Horizontal	*Vertical*	*Gun turrets*	*Con. tower*	*Engine output S.H.P.*	*Speed kn*	*Fuel ts*	*Radius of action, s.m. at a speed of kn*
32-33	Wyoming	76	38-279	279-305	229-305	28 000	20,5	5 100	8 000/11
34-35	New York	95	38-305	229-305	152-305	28 100	21	5 200	9 000/11
36-37	Nevada	51-76	57-343	127-406	343-406	N=26 500 O=24 800	20	5 300	10 000/11
38-39	Pennsylvania	51-102	57-356	127-457	356-406	P=31 500 A=33 500	21 21	5 000	8 000/12

Construction data, armor, and propulsion

Penn. No.	Name of the ship	F.Y.	Laid down	Launched	Commissioned	Decommissioned	Paid off	Build. Yard	Fate
40	New Mexico	14	14.10.15	23. 4.17	20. 5.18	19. 7.46	25. 2.47	New York Nav.Sh.	Scrapped
41	Mississippi	14	5. 4.15	25. 1.17	18.12.17	as AG: 17.9.56	12.56	Newport News S.B.&D.D.	Scrapped
42	Idaho	14	20. 1.15	30. 6.17	24. 3.19	3. 7.46	6. 9.47	New York S.B.,Camden	Scrapped
43	Tennessee	15	14. 5.17	30. 4.19	3. 6.20	14. 2.47	1. 3.59	New York Nav.Sh.	Scrapped
44	California	15	25.10.16	20.11.19	10. 8.21	7. 8.46	1. 3.59	Mare Island Nav.Sh.	Scrapped
45	Colorado	16	29. 5.19	22. 3.21	30. 8.23	7. 1.47	1. 3.59	New York S.B.,Camden	Scrapped
46	Maryland	16	24. 4.17	20. 3.20	21. 7.21	3. 4.47	1. 3.59	Newport News S.B.&D.D.	Scrapped
47	Washington	16	30. 6.19	1. 9.21	11/24	construction canc.		New York S.B.,Camden	Sunk as a target
48	West Virginia	16	12. 4.20	19.11.21	1.12.23	9. 1.47	1. 3.59	Newport News S.B.&D.D.	Scrapped
49	South Dakota	17	15. 3.20	8. 2.22	construction canc.			New York Nav.Sh.	Scrapped
50	Indiana	17	1.11.20	8. 2.22	construction canc.			New York Nav.Sh.	Scrapped
51	Montana	17	1. 9.20	8. 2.22	construction canc.			Mare Island Nav.Sh.	Scrapped
52	North Carolina	18	12. 1.20	8. 2.22	construction canc.			Norfolk Nav. Sh.	Scrapped
53	Iowa	18	17. 5.20	8. 2.22	construction canc.			Newport News S.B.&D.D.	Scrapped
54	Massachusetts	18	4. 4.21	8. 2.22	construction canc.			Fore River, Quincy	Scrapped

BB	Class	Armor in mm								
		Horizontal	*Vertical*	*Gun turrets*	*Con. tower*	*Engine output S.H.P.*	*Speed kn*	*Fuel ts*	*Radius of action, s.m. at a speed of kn*
40-42	New Mexico	51-127	57-356	127-457	356-406	40 000	21,5	5 500	9 000/12
43-44	Tennessee	127	57-356	127-457	356-406	30 000	T=21 C=20,5	T=4 900 C=5 500	T= 9 000/12 C=10 000/12
45-48	Colorado	102	57-406	127-457	203-406	34 000	21	4 500 WV=5 500	WV=10 000/12 8 000/12
49-54	South Dakota I	64-152	343	127-457	406	60 000	23		

Construction data, armor, and propulsion

Penn. No.	Name of the ship	F.Y.	Laid down	Launched	Commissioned	Decommissioned	Paid off	Build, Yard	Fate
CC/1	Lexington	16	8. 1.21	als CV/2q completed as CV 2				Fore River, Quincy	War loss 1942
CC 2	Constellation	16	18. 8.20	17. 8.23	construction canc.			Newport News S.B.&D.D.	Broken up
CC 3	Saratoga	16	25. 9.20	als CV 3	completed as CV 3			New York S.B.,Camden	Sunk as a target for nuclear test
CC 4	Ranger	16	23. 6.21	17. 8.23	construction canc.			Newport News S.B.&D.D.	Broken up
CC 5	Constitution	17	25. 9.20	17. 8.23	construction canc.			Philadelphia Nav. Sh.	Broken up
CC 6	United States	19	29. 9.20	17. 8.23	construction canc.			Philadelphia Nav. Sh.	Broken up
55	North Carolina	37	27.10.37	13. 6.40	9. 4.41	27. 6.47	1. 6.60	New York Nav. Sh.	Now relic at Wilmington, N.C.
56	Washington	37	14. 6.38	1. 6.40	15. 5.41	27. 6.47	1. 6.60	Philadelphia Nav. Sh.	Scrapped
57	South Dakota	38	5. 7.39	7. 6.41	20. 3.42	31. 1.47	1. 6.62	New York S.B.,Camden	Scrapped
58	Indiana	38	20.11.39	21.11.41	30. 4.42	11. 9.46	1. 6.62	Newport News S.B.&D.D.	Scrapped
59	Massachusetts	38	20. 7.39	23. 9.41	12. 5.42	27. 3.47	1. 6.62	Bethlehem, Quincy	Now relic at Fall River, Mass.
60	Alabama	38	1. 2.40	16. 2.42	16. 8.42	9. 1.47	1. 6.62	Norfolk Nav. Sh.	Now relic at Mobile, Ala.

BB	Class	Armor in mm							
		Horizontal	*Vertical*	*Gun turrets*	*Con. tower*	*Engine Output S.H.P.*	*Speed kn*	*Fuel ts*	*Radius of action, s.m. at a speed of kn*
CC 1-6	Lexington	32-57	178	356	406	180 000	33,2		
55-56	North Carolina	117	25-305	178-406 19- 25	178-373	121 000	28	6 590	12 000/12
57-60	Dakota II South	127	25-305	184-457 19- 25	203-406	130 000	28	$\{\begin{matrix} A=6\ 975 \\ I=7\ 340 \end{matrix}$ $\{\begin{matrix} SD \\ M \end{matrix}\}=6\ 950$	$\{\begin{matrix} A \\ \end{matrix}=14\ 000/12$ $\{\begin{matrix} SD \\ M \end{matrix}=12\ 000/12$

Construction data, armor, and propulsion

Penn. No.	Name of the ship	F.Y.	Laid down	Launched	Commissioned	Decommissioned	Build. Yard	Fate
61	Iowa	40	27. 6.40	27. 8.42	22. 2.43 24. 8.51	24. 3.49 24. 2.58	New York Nav. Sh.	1976 in Reserve Fleet
62	New Jersey	40	16. 9.40	7.12.42	23. 5.43 21.11.50 8. 4.68	30. 6.48 21. 8.57 17.12.69	Philadelphia Nav. Sh.	1976 in Reserve Fleet
63	Missouri	40	6. 1.41	29. 1.44	11. 6.44	26. 2.55	New York Nav. Sh.	1976 in Reserve Fleet
64	Wisconsin	40	25. 1.41	7.12.43	16. 4.44 3. 3.51	1. 7.48 8. 3.58	Philadelphia Nav. Sh.	1976 in Reserve Fleet
65	Illinois	40	15. 1.45	12. 8.45	construction canc.		Philadelphia Nav. Sh.	Broken up
66	Kentucky	40	6.12.44	20. 1.50	construction canc.		Norfolk Nav. Sh.	Broken up
67	Montana	40	21. 7.43	construction canc.			Philadelphia Nav. Sh.	
68	Ohio	40	21. 7.43	construction canc.			Philadelphia Nav. Sh.	
69	Maine	40	21. 7.43	construction canc.			New York Nav. Sh.	
70	New Hampshire	40	21. 7.43	construction canc.			New York Nav. Sh.	
71	Louisiana	40	21. 7.43	construction canc.			Norfolk Nav. Sh.	

BB	Class	Horizontal	Vertical	Gun turrets	Con. tower	Engine output S.H.P.	Speed kn	Fuel ts	Radius of action, s.m. at a speed of kn
61-66	Iowa	142	310	184-496 19- 25	280-445	212 000	33	7 250 I=7 100	15 000/12
67-71	Montana	154	457	197-534	197-457	172 000	28		

Technical data and armament

| Penn. No. | Name of the ship | Displacement | | Height | | Length | Beam | Draught | Complement | |
		Standard ts	Full load ts	Bow Stack m	Stern Mast m	m	m	m	Peace	War
32	Wyoming 1945:	19.700				170,3	28,4	8,7	as BB: 1 063	as AG: 400
33	Arkansas	26.100	31.000	8,2 22,0	6,1 31,4	170,3	32,2	9,7	1 330	1 650
34	New York	27.000	32.000	7,6 22,0	5,5 41,2	174,7	32,4	9,6	1 340	1 530
35	Texas	27.000	32.000	7,6 22,0	5,5 41,2	174,7	32,4	9,6	1 340	1 530
36	Nevada	29.000	34.000	8,4 29,3 1943 after	4,9 36,9 conversion	177,8	32,9	9,9	1 301	
37	Oklahoma	29.000	28.900			177,8	29,0	8,7	864	1 025
38	Pennsylvania	33.100	36.500	7,9 23,2	4,6 38,7	185,3	32,4	10,2	1 358	2 290
39	Arizona	32.600	36.500	7,9 23,2	4,6 38,7	185,3	29,6	8,8	1 358	2 290

Year	Armament heavy battery	secondary battery	A.A. guns	Catap.	Aircr.	Notes
1932	6-12in-L/50₂	16-5in-L/25₁	8-3in-L/25₁	—	—	After May 1931 gunnery training ship = AG 17
1944	—	—	10-5in-L/38 4-3in 11-40mm	—	—	After 1944 A.A. training ship; armament changed occasionally
1934	12-12in-L/50₂	16-5in-L/51₁	8-3in-L/50₁	1	3	5in partly in casemates
1942	12-12in-L/50₂	6-5in-L/51₁	10-3in 32/36-40mm 26/20	1	3	
1937	10-14in-L/45₂	16-5in-L/51₁	8-3in-L/50₁ 8-2, 8cm			5in partly in casemates
1942	10-14in-L/45₂	6-5in-L/51₁	10-3in-L/50₁ 24/40-40mm 42/36-20mm	1	3	20-mm-A.A. guns reduced
1937	10-14in-L/45₂	16-5in-L/51₁	8-3in-L/50₁ 8-2,8cm	1	3	5in in casemates
1942	10-14in-L/45₂	6-5in-L/51₁	10-3in-L/50₁ 24/40-40mm 42/36-20mm	1	3	20-mm-A.A. guns reduced
1935	10-14in-L/45₂₊₃	12-5in-L/51₁	8-5in-L/25₁	2	3	5in-L/51 in casemates
1942	10-14in-L/45₂₊₃	—	16-5in-L/38₂ 36-40mm maximum 38-20mm	1	3	
1935	10-14in-L/45₂₊₃	12-5in-L/51₁	8-5in-L/25₁	2	3	5in-L/51 in casemates. Sunk at Pearl Harbor
1940	12-14in-L/45₃	12-5in-L/51₁	12-5in-L/25₁ 8-2,8cm	2	3	5in-L/51 in casemates
1943	12-14in-L/45₃		16-5in-L/38₂ 40/45-40mm maximum 50-20mm	1	3	
1940	12-14in-L/45₃	12-5in-L/51₁	12-5in-L/25₁	2	3	5in-L/51 in casemates

Technical data and armament

Penn. No.	Name of the ship	Displacement		Height		Length	Beam	Draught	Complement	
		Standard ts	Full load ts	Bow Stack m	Stern Mast m	m	m	m	Peace	War
40	New Mexico	33.400	36.000	7,3 25,3	4,6 36,0	190,2	32,4	10,4	1 323	1 930
41	Mississippi	33.000	35.100	7,3 25,3	4,6 36,0	190,7	32,4	10,4	1 323	1 930
42	Idaho	33.400	36.000	7,3 25,3	4,6 36,0	190,2	32,4	10,4	1 323	1 930
43	Tennessee	32.300	35.190	8,2 28,4	5,2 37,5	190,4	29,7 (34,8) (after conversion)	9,2	1 480	2 375
44	California	32.600	35.190	8,2 28,4	5,2 37,5	190,4	29,7 (34,8) (after conversion)	9,2	1 480	2 375
45	Colorado	35.000	40.396	7,2 21,7	4,6 38,7	190,4	32,9	10,7	1 407	1 968
46	Maryland	34.000	39.100	7,2 21,7	4,6 38,7	190,2	32,9	10,7	1 407	1 968
48	West Virginia	37.800	40.354	8,2 28,4 1944 after conversion	5,2 37,5	190,2	34,8	10,8	1 486	2 182

Year	Armament heavy battery	secondary battery	A.A. guns	Catap.	Aircr.	Notes
1940	12-14in-L/50$_3$	12-5in-L/51$_1$	8-5in-L/25$_1$ 12-2,8cm	2	3	10-5in-L/51 in casemates
1943	12-14in-L/50$_3$		8-5in-L/25$_1$ 40-40mm 34-20mm	1	3	
1940	12-14in-L/50$_3$	12-5in-L/51$_1$	8-5in-L/25$_1$ 12-2,8cm	2	3	10-5in-L/51 in casemates
1945	12-14in-L/50$_3$		14-5in-L/25$_1$ 56-40mm 9-20mm	1	3	
1940	12-14in-L/50$_3$	12-5in-L/51$_1$	8-5in-L/25$_1$ 12-2,8cm	2	3	10-5in-L/51 in casemates
1945	12-14in-L/50$_3$		10-5in-L/38$_1$ 40-40mm 29-20mm	1	3	
1936	12-14in-L/50$_3$	12-5in-L/51$_1$	8-5in-L/25$_1$ 11-2,8cm	2	3	10-5in-L/51 in casemates
1945	12-14in-L/50$_3$		16-5in-L/38$_2$ 40-40mm 41-20mm	1	3	
1936	12-14in-L/50$_3$	12-5in-L/51$_1$	8-5in-L/25$_1$ 11-2,8cm	2	3	10-5in-L/51 in casemates
1945	12-14in-L/50$_3$		16-5in-L/38$_2$ 56-40mm 31-20mm	1	3	
1938	8-16in-L/45$_2$	12-5in-L/51$_1$	8-5in-L/25$_1$ 11-2,8cm	2	3	5in-L/51 in casemates
1945	8-16in-L/45$_2$	8-5in-L/51$_1$	8-5in-L/38$_1$ 40-40mm 33-20mm	1	3	
1938	8-16in-L/45$_2$	12-5in-L/51$_1$	8-5in-L/25$_1$ 11-2,8cm	2	3	5in-L/51 in casemates, prior to 1945 37-20mm
1945	8-16in-L/45$_2$		16-5in-L/38$_2$ 40-40mm 18-20mm	1	3	
1938	8-16in-L/45$_2$	12-5in-L/51$_1$	8-5in-L/25$_1$ 11-2,8cm	2	3	5in-L/51 in casemates
1944	8-16in-L/45$_2$		16-5in-L/38$_2$ 40-40mm 50-20mm	1	3	

Technical data and armament

Penn. No.	Name of the ship	Displacement		Height Bow Stack m	Stern Mast m	Length	Beam	Draught	Complement	
		Standard ts	Full load ts			m	m	m	Peace	War
49-54	South Dakota (Class)	43.200	47.000			208,5	32,2	10,0	1 470	
CC 1-6	Lexington (Class)	43.500 third design	49.000			266,5	32,2	9,1	1 315	
55	North Carolina	38.000	46.770	9,5 26,8	6,1 37,2	222,1	32,9	10,7	1 880	2 339
56	Washington	38.000	45.370	9,5 26,8	6,1 37,2	222,2	33,0	10,7	1 880	2 339
57	South Dakota	38.000	44.374	8,8 24,7	6,7 40,6	207,5	32,9	11,0	1 793	2 354
58	Indiana	38.000	44.374	8,8 24,7	6,7 40,6	207,5	32,9	11,0	1 793	2 354
59	Massachusetts	38.000	45.216	8,8 24,7	6,7 40,6	207,3	32,9	11,0	1 793	2 354
60	Alabama	38.000	44.374	8,8 24,7	6,7 40,6	207,5	32,9	11,0	1 793	2 354
61	Iowa	48.500	57.450	11,0 29,9	6,7 40,9	270,5	33,0	11,0	1 921	2 978
62	New Jersey	48.500	57.450 (1968: 54.000)	11,0 29,9	6,7 40,9	270,6	33,0	11,0	1 921	2 978 1968: 1 556
63	Missouri	48.500	57.216	11,0 29,9	6,7 40,9	270,5	33,0	11,0	1 921	2 978
64	Wisconsin	48.500	57.216	11,0 29,9	6,7 40,9	270,6	33,0	11,0	1 921	2 978
67-71	Montana (Class)	60.500	70.500			280,9	36,9	11,0		3 000

Year	Armament heavy battery	secondary battery	A.A. guns	Catap.	Aircr.	Notes
	12-16in-L/50₃	16-6in-L/53₁	6-3in	—	—	6in in casemates two 21in torpedo tubes
	8-16in-L/50₂	16-6in-L/53₁	6-3in	1	1	Armament third design; 8-6in in casemates; eight 21in torpedo tubes
1943	9-16in-L/45₃		20-5in-L/38₂)96-40mm)54-20mm	2	3	
1943	9-16in-L/45₃		20-5in-L/38₂)60-40mm maxim.)54-20mm	2	3	
1943	9-16in-L/45₃		16-5in-L/38₂)60-40mm maxim.)54-20mm	2	3	
1943	9-16in-L/45₃		20-5in-L/38₂ 32-40mm 40-20mm	2	3	
1943	9-16in-L/45₃		20-5in-L/38₂ 64-40mm 30-20mm	2	3	
1943	9-16in-L/45₃		20-5in-L/38₂ 48-40mm 42-20mm	2	3	
1944	9-16in-L/50₃		20-5in-L/38₂ 60-40mm 60-20mm	2	4	Ending with 56-40mm only
1944	9-16in-L/50₃		20-5in-L/38₂ 62-40mm 60-20mm	2	4	Ending with 56-40mm only
1968	9-16in-L/50₃		20-5in-L/38₂		2Hel.	
1944	9-16in-L/50₃		20-5in-L/38₂ 80-40mm 49-20mm	2	4	Ending with 56-40mm only
1944	9-16in-L/50₃		20-5in-L/38₂ 80-40mm 49-20mm	2	4	Ending with 56-40mm only
	12-16in-L/50₃		20-5in-L/54₂ 40-40mm 48-20mm	2	4	